A ROCK GARDEN HANDBOOK FOR BEGINNERS

Published by
The North American
Rock Garden Society

Edited by Jack Ferreri

January 1999

Cover illustration, **sand bed in the Slater garden.** *Photo by Michael Slater*

Copyright 1999 by the North American Rock Garden Society

Printed by AgPress, 1531 Yuma Street, Manhattan, KS 66505

TABLE OF CONTENTS

Introduction

The North American Rock Garden Society contains a vast collection of "received wisdom." Past and present growers of these mountain plants have decades of experience to draw on … their own successes and failures, those of their friends, trips to the mountains, and lectures or published materials.

Beginners starting to grow unusual plants like those found in the typical rock garden often face challenges in mastering the basics. Most local gardeners don't know much about *Draba* or *Androsace*. Area nurseries usually can't provide any help with alpine primroses or the many dwarf *Potentilla*. The palette of the rock gardener is vast and brilliant, but the novice often finds it challenging to get the first few strokes of color onto the canvas.

A Rock Garden Handbook for Beginners is designed to help newcomers to the world of rock or alpine gardening get their bearings. We've drawn on our richest resource—the back issues of our flagship publication, the *Rock Garden Quarterly*. Published since 1943, it has provided rock gardeners over the years with hundreds of instructive articles on every aspect of alpine plants and their culture.

This booklet opens with several fundamental articles describing what sets rock gardening apart from other gardens, as well as time-tested advice on how to build a good one. You'll then see some special growing techniques rock gardeners have developed to give the plants the special conditions they need … the scree, raised beds, stone walls, and sand beds. Since many rock gardeners have a passion for woodland and shade plants, we include an article on how to create a perfect habitat for woodlanders. Finally, we include a lengthy listing of plants with which newcomers will have the best luck. The booklet concludes with a list of resources you can turn to for more information.

Mountain plants brings a special feeling to the garden—with their wild heritage and their singular beauty. This booklet shares with you how some very accomplished growers have found ways to make these plants flourish for all of us.

Jack Ferreri, Editor

Rock and Alpine Gardens

by T. H. Everett

Gardens in which rocks and plants appropriate to them are the chief landscape elements are called rock gardens. If the plants are entirely or mainly sorts to grow naturally at higher altitudes or under subarctic or arctic conditions, such gardens are sometimes called alpine gardens. Well planned and well executed rock gardens are esthetically agreeable as well as horticulturally stimulating.

Joy of Rock Gardening

The satisfactions of rock gardening lie not alone in creating and maintaining pleasing landscapes, but also in developing intimate acquaintance with and caring for the plants accommodated. At its best, rock gardening is a splendid hobby, not excessively demanding, yet sufficiently challenging to reward reasonable dedication and attention. Because the plants used are chiefly small, many sorts can be accommodated in quite limited areas. This appeals to gardeners with a well-developed instinct for collecting, a commendable expression of horticultural interest displayed by many amateurs.

Another attraction of rock gardening is that, apart from initial construction perhaps, the tasks connected with it are generally light and agreeable. Most can be accomplished while puttering around the garden at longer periods on more fixed time schedules as some other types of gardening demand.

English Rock Gardens

Historically, rock gardening began in the British Isles, its development an outcome of the greatly increased numbers of travelers from there who from early in the nineteenth century on visited Switzerland and other mountainous parts in Europe. Enamored by the great wealth of beautiful alpine plants they saw, unknown in their own countries, they were inspired to bring some back and attempt to grow them at home.

Because of a nearly complete lack of understanding of the needs of alpine and other mountain plants, most early attempts at domesticating them were dismal failures. A few of the toughest and more adaptable sorts survived in the generally atrocious "rockeries" built by Victorians, but in the main those horticultural conceits, which sometimes included grottos, arches, bridges, and other elaborate architectural features, became graveyards for the choicer alpines enthusiasts had plucked from their mountain homes.

But gradually improvement came. As early as 1870, William Robinson, in his book *Alpine Flowers for English Gardens*, attempted to give some guidance, and by the early years of the twentieth century, an altogether better appreciation of the needs of mountain plants had developed and skills in cultivating them improved. Nevertheless, for a long time, rock gardens continued to be poorly made and many esthetically unsatisfactory ones were established, as, sadly, are some modern ones. The least attractive belong in the groups the inspired English authority Reginald Farrer characterized as the almond pudding, dog's grave, and devil's lapful styles and that later in America became known as peanut brittle rock gardens.

Before the end of the first decade of the twentieth century, capable Europeans were advocating sound principles for constructing and planting rock gardens and for caring for plants appropriate to them. Among the books in that decade are *My Rock Garden*, by Reginald Farrer, whose famous garden was in Yorkshire, England, and *Rock Gardens* by Lewis Meredith, who gardened in County Wicklow, Ireland.

Completed in 1913, but not published until six years later, Farrer's book *The English Rock Garden* became the bible of rock gardeners everywhere. A master of English prose, the author stimulated thousands to attempt the cultivation of the plants he so beautifully, entrancingly, and sometimes extravagantly described.

Another benchmark was the publication, in English in 1930, of *Rock Garden and Alpine Plants* by Henri Correvon, the distinguished Swiss pioneer in the cultivation of alpine plants. As early as 1877, Correvon exhibited at a horticultural flower show in Geneva a small collection of alpines he had grown from seeds, for which pains he was accounted a "young enthusiast who does not realize the needs of the gardening world." Nevertheless, at the urging of one of the judges who thought the Société d' Horticulture de Genève should "give him something as evidence that the Société is interested in encouraging young beginners," Correvon was awarded a prize, four little silver teaspoons.

American Rock Gardens

In North America, interest in rock gardens began later than in Europe, yet in 1890 an example patterned after that at the Royal Botanic Gardens, Kew, England, but much smaller, was constructed at Smith College Botanic Garden, Northampton, Massachusetts. In the 1920s, another was installed at the Brooklyn Botanic Garden in New York City, and in 1932, construction began on the Thompson Memorial Rock Garden [*Ed. Note: now the T. H. Everett Rock Garden*] at The New York Botanical Garden in New York City.

Meanwhile, keen amateurs were furthering the cause of rock gardening on both coasts of America. The publication in 1923 of Louise Beebe Wilder's delightful book The Rock Garden and the many other writings of this competent cultivator and talented author stimulated many Americans to engage in the new hobby.

Other circumstances that in the period between the two world wars encouraged the rapid expansion of enthusiasm for rock gardening were the organization of the American Rock Garden Society and the truly marvelous examples of planted rock gardens staged as exhibits at the great spring flower shows in Boston, New York and Philadelphia, by the superb artists of rock garden design and construction, Marcel LePiniec, Ralph Hancock, and Zenon Schrieber. The American Rock Garden Society continues to flourish and to attract to its membership people interested in its special field. [*Ed. note: the American Rock Garden Society, ARGS, was renamed North American Rock Garden Society, NARGS, in 1994.*]

Partly because of climate, which in many parts of North America precludes or makes extremely difficult the cultivation of many true alpines that are the glories of European rock gardens, and partly because of the availability of numerous charming small plants native to the continent that are not alpines, most American rock gardeners wisely do not limit their plantings to inhabitants of high mountains, but include other neat and choice kinds that look as if they properly belong. And this is as it should be.

Climate and Plants

Traditionally, and as generally interpreted, rock gardening involves the cultivation of mountain plants and other low sorts that withstand severe winter cold with impunity and is thought of as belonging only in temperate climates.

But viewed as an art form based on the agreeable use of rocks in the landscape, the development of rock gardens is as appropriate in warm temperate, subtropical, and tropical climates as in temperate ones. Certainly there are many places in such regions where cliffs, outcropping rocks, and similar formations are as inspiring as those of colder regions, and the principles of adapting or constructing such features as garden landscapes are not different.

The kinds of plants to employ in warm climates quite obviously differ from those useful in colder ones, but plenty are available. Fit choices to local conditions. In desert and semidesert areas, cactuses and other succulents in nearly endless array are obvious possibilities. They look especially well in association with rocks. For humid warm climate regions, there are available just as many sorts of plants appropriate for displaying in rock environments. They include ferns, as well as many kinds of begonias, gesneriads, peperomias, and other plants, many of which as wildlings inhabit cliffs and other rock features.

There are two chief types of rock gardens, natural and artificial. The first represents the development of sites on which native rocks are prominent as outcrops, cliffs, or perhaps strewn boulders. The others are made in areas in which all or most of the rocks used must be imported.

Existence of a site of the first description is reason enough for adapting it as a rock garden, but constructed gardens are generally only justified by a genuine desire to grow and display small plants the majority of which are not well suited for flower beds and borders. There are sometimes rockless sites, such as banks and steep slopes, where the development of a rock garden presents fewer problems than other treatments.

Getting Started

To begin a natural rock garden, first make a careful survey of the site and identify the plants growing there. Some especially well-located, deep-rooted trees such as oaks and hickories that can be relied upon to provide light shade for part or all of each day in summer, besides adding to the charm and perhaps majesty of the area, should be preserved, but remove overcrowded, spindly specimens and weedy sorts of little garden merit along with tangles of brushwood and similar undesirable growth. There may be too, evergreen or deciduous shrubs or herbaceous perennials, such as ferns, bulbs, and other wildlings, that should be retained where they are or transplanted elsewhere.

Clearing the area of unwanted vegetation may then be done by digging out completely all roots as well as tops. Then give attention to any pruning retained trees and shrubs need. Cut out all dead and seriously diseased wood and, if desirable, thin out branches from dense specimens. It is often advantageous to provide for more side light by removing some lower branches to "raise the heads" of trees that cast too dense shade.

Rearrangement of a few rocks, or even supplementing those on the site with others brought in, is permissible, but it must be done so skillfully that even persons knowledgeable about natural formations cannot easily detect the artifice. Transported rocks must match precisely those of the site and be positioned as though placed by nature.

Soil

Improving the soil is the next order of business. Unless you are dedicated to growing plants that need quite different types of soil than what you have, do not attempt drastic changes in its basic character. For example, if it is naturally acid or alkaline, accept the condition and select plants adapted to it. Concentrate on bettering soil texture where needed by mixing in such additives as chips of crushed rock, coarse sand, perlite, or, for alkaline soil plants, crushed limestone or crushed clam or oyster shells. For woodland or moorland plants, add generous amounts of leafmold, peat moss, compost, or similar organic material.

Make certain there is adequate depth of soil, especially in the crevices and crannies you intend to plant. It is usually desirable to rake out existing soil and, if necessary after deepening or enlarging the clefts or crevices, to replace it with a better mix, firmly packed, so no voids are left.

Planting is best done in early fall or early spring, but not until disturbed ground has had time to settle or before it is reasonably certain that it is essentially free of pestiferous perennial weeds. Whenever practicable, it is advantageous to allow an entire growing season to elapse between the preparation of the site and actual planting. This permits clearing the soil of weeds and ensuring clean planting areas by pulling up or hoeing off every one as soon as it shows above ground.

Plants and Placement

The sorts of plants appropriate for natural rock gardens are likely to include many native to the region as well as others that thrive under similar conditions. In selected spots and corners, avid rock gardeners are likely to try a few more challenging sorts.

To be convincing, placement of the plants calls for an appreciation of how vegetation is disposed on natural rocky sites. Seek inspiration from such places, noting the unstrained informality that prevails. Here, irregular drifts of low plants may carpet the soil surface or occupy ledges, shelves, or miniature plateaus, with very likely outlying smaller groups or individuals, often at lower levels or to the lee of the main groups, the outcome of seeds that have fallen and been washed away or have drifted down from the main colonies. Note how plants run along narrow crevices or congregate at the bases of miniature cliffs. Without slavishly copying such native features, let your natural rock garden epitomize them and represent a distillation of what is good about what you find in the wild, miniaturized and tailored to accommodate the plants you want to grow.

Rocks and Garden Construction

Rock gardens constructed on sites devoid of native rock or where little is present clearly offer opportunities for imaginative development, yet in such places the most inappropriate examples amusingly characterized by Reginald Farrer, are often perpetrated.

Following Farrer's castigation, the better examples of British rock gardens were made in what their builders fondly imagined was a natural fashion, but because many of those who made such gardens failed to study rock formations as they occur in the wild, they were usually unconvincing.

At first, great emphasis was placed on creating "pockets" to be planted with individual kinds of plants and the structure was likely to consist of a series of such little flat or nearly flat terraces backed by and supported by more or less vertical walls of stone. Such was the rock garden at the Royal Botanic Garden, Kew, England, until the 1930s, and many others constructed in Great Britain and elsewhere followed the same general plan. The pockets, frequently referred to in garden writings of the time, were well drained and bottomless so the soil with which they were filled connected directly with the main body of earth beneath and made it entirely practicable for plants to grow and flourish, but the overall esthetic effect was rarely satisfactory. But gradually improvements came, and between the two world wars, gardens more suggestive of native rock formations were developed both in Europe and America.

Choosing the Site

The choice of a site for a rock garden may be wide or limited depending upon the extent and character of the property. The advice so often given in older writings to locate the garden well out of sight of buildings and other formal features, is, on small grounds, often not tenable, and certainly is not essential to success in cultivating alpines and other rock garden plants.

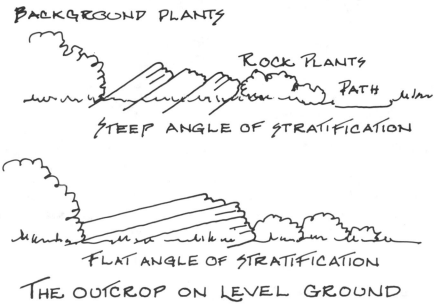

BACKGROUND PLANTS

ROCK PLANTS

PATH

STEEP ANGLE OF STRATIFICATION

FLAT ANGLE OF STRATIFICATION

THE OUTCROP ON LEVEL GROUND

It is by no means necessary to duplicate or even approximate an alpine scene to achieve a satisfying and beautiful rock garden. Such styles may be admirable in suitable surroundings, but so are rock gardens of other types. It is even possible to install a garden adjacent to a building or cropping out of a lawn without being incongruous, possibilities earlier advocates of rock gardens and some contemporaries completely reject. Furthermore, garden features suitable for embellishment with rock plants that make no pretense of naturalness, and yet are congruous and beautiful, can be developed. To this category belong what are known as dry walls, of which more will be discussed later.

A secret of success of rock gardens that aspire to naturalness, be they near or remote from manmade structures, be they large or small, is the placement of the rocks. To be convincing the effect must be that they were positioned by nature without aid from man. Here, if ever, true art is to conceal art.

The surest ways of obtaining such effects are (1) to use the same type of rock throughout the garden or at least throughout major parts of it, (2) to position each piece so that it appears stable and, except for minor crevices, connected with neighboring pieces above ground such that the whole apparently represents the exposed part of a massive underground formation, and (3) if the rock be stratified, to lay the pieces with the strata lines all in one direction. Granted, because of geological or other disturbances the disposition of rocks in the wild does not always conform to these principles, the departure from them, unless carried out very skillfully by one who has carefully studied natural deviations from them, is very likely to produce uneasy unconvincing effects.

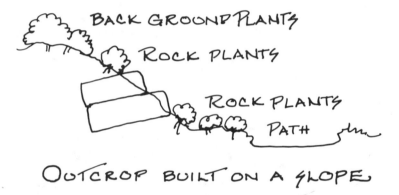

OUTCROP BUILT ON A SLOPE

Especially appropriate sites for rock gardens are slopes, banks, and small valleys or dells, natural or created, but flat areas can also be utilized. A first necessity is to evaluate the area, particularly with reference to any contouring that may be desirable. If a pool, stream, or waterfall is contemplated, and these can add greatly to the charms of rock gardens. Their locations and courses must be planned, and so, especially if the garden is sizable, must be paths needed to enjoy and service the area.

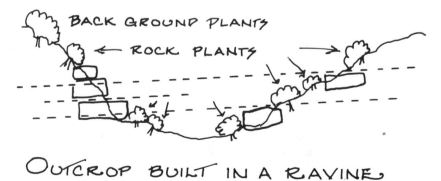

OUTCROP BUILT IN A RAVINE

Contouring is usually best achieved by stripping and stockpiling the topsoil, fashioning the undersoil to the convolutions and grades deemed appropriate (this may involve bringing in additional material), then after modifying it in any way that seems desirable, and if necessary supplying additional soil to achieve a depth of at least one foot, replacing the topsoil. Modification, if the soil is not sufficiently porous, will involve mixing in generous amounts of coarse sand, grit, or small chips of stone, and if woodland plants are to be grown probably the admixture of leaf mold, peat moss, or other suitable partially decayed organic material. If a section of the garden is to be devoted to plants that need alkaline soil, crushed limestone or limestone chips may be included in the topsoil mix.

Finding the Best Rocks

The kind of rock used is usually determined by availability. Where choice may be had, one that is porous, rather than such hard, impervious types as granite and schist, is to be preferred. Hard sandstones, and not excessively soluble limestones are very satisfactory. But remember, limestones, and waterworn limestone is one of the most beautiful rocks, are distasteful or unacceptable to such acid soil plants as heaths, heathers, and rhododendrons. Tufa, a soft, lightweight, porous limestone-type rock formed by calcium carbonate deposited in springs and streams, is easy to handle and congenial to plants, but of undistinguished appearance. Harder rocks can be used, but take longer to weather because they are less encouraging to the growth of mosses, lichens, and other primitive vegetation that soon conceals freshly exposed portions of softer rocks.

Unless no other is available, do not use newly quarried rock. Its raw surfaces are likely to take a long time to weather and, even worse, may display marks of drilling. Weathered pieces collected from the surface of the ground and of a character and color that suggest age are likely to be ideal. In some parts of the country suitable material can be obtained from old stone walls. The pieces must be of manageable sizes and of acceptable relation to the size of the garden, although here some "cheating" can be done for, by careful placement, it is possible to arrange several comparatively small rocks so skillfully that they appear to be a creviced bigger one. When the chinks between them are filled with plants that effect is greatly enhanced.

Boulders are generally considered unsatisfactory for rock gardens, and certainly they should not be mixed with angular rocks, but if boulders are all that is available it is not impossible to fashion a convincing garden from them as was done at the Brooklyn Botanic Garden.

The secret is to use boulders of different sizes and to position them, some partly buried, some exposed, as they would be in the bed of a dry stream or wash. Let the areas between the stones slope gently except for some accumulations of what represent washed-down, stony, gravelly, sandy soil piled on the "upstream" side of boulders. These accumulations may be level-topped or even tilted slightly against the prevailing slope.

Take care not to scar rocks when collecting and handling them. To minimize the danger it may be worthwhile wrapping choice pieces in burlap. Use crowbars, often necessary for levering large pieces, although sometimes staves of wood or pieces of two-by-four can be used for this purpose, with care to avoid bruising the rock. If possible have rocks delivered to the tops of slopes. It is easier to move them downhill than up.

Spacing the Rocks

When constructing the garden, do not distribute the rock evenly throughout; instead, make massive use of it in some parts, employ it sparingly or not at all in others. Take a cue from natural rocky places where accumulations of detritus and washed or blown soil form slopes and terraces about and between bold protrusions of rock. In gardens, rockless areas afford relief to the eye, splendid opportunities for planting attractively, and by contrast give seemingly greater massiveness and importance to the rocky portions.

Areas that lend themselves to rocklessness or to not more than suspicions of rock poking through the surface are gentle slopes downward and backward from the tops of cliffs, moraine-type slopes forward and downward from the fronts of cliffs, valley-like depressions between outcrops, and little flats bordering streams and pools.

Installing Special Features

Install the most massive features of the garden first. These may include bold outcrops, cliffs, and perhaps a waterfall. Give special attention to the location of the last as well as to other water features. Water spouting from the top of a hill or cliff is all wrong; it lacks the appearance of naturalness. To seem plausible, there must be, or by skillful construction or planting the viewer must be led to believe there is, a catchment area of considerable size above the point of emergence to account for the volume of water.

Pools and watercourses call for special thought. The supply may be natural, piped in, or recycled by a pump. If artificial, be sure its source is concealed. With careful planning, a comparatively small flow can be managed so that it is seen more than once to give the impression that the garden is much better supplied with water than it really is.

Placing the Rocks

When placing the rocks begin at the low parts of slopes and work upward, carefully setting each piece with its most attractive weathered side exposed and, so far as consistent with naturalness, with its top sloped slightly backward to direct rain or water from sprinklers to the roots. With this same thought in mind, avoid overhangs that keep water from reaching rock faces below them.

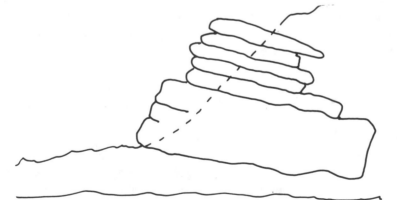

USING THIN STONES TO FORM A STRATA

Strive to achieve a feeling of stability. Leave no impression that the rocks are separate pieces susceptible to being easily loosened and removed. This is most surely done, so far as practicable, by setting each with its broadest side as its base, a positioning that suggests the most common aspect of exposed portions of outcropping rocks and the usual attitude of surface rocks in the wild. To achieve stability, with the rocks in their best possible positions, it is sometimes desirable to prop a large rock on several smaller ones and then to fill the voids with firmly packed soil.

A variation of this procedure that, if skillfully done, carries conviction and is highly satis-factory, is to stand flat rocks, much thinner than long or wide, on edge with their most attractive broad sides facing outward to form miniature cliffs. In this way height is achieved with much less bulk of stone than is required if one or two or more superimposed pieces are set widest side down to produce similar effects. When using such rocks take special care to set them in positions of repose that allow of no easy disturbance. This is particularly important in regions where strong outward thrusting comes from the soil freezing deeply.

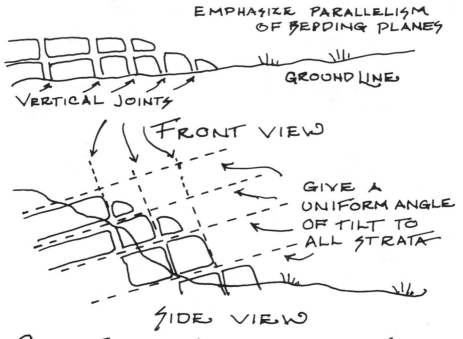

EMPHASIZE PARALLELISM
OF BEDDING PLANES

GROUND LINE

VERTICAL JOINTS

FRONT VIEW

GIVE A
UNIFORM ANGLE
OF TILT TO
ALL STRATA

SIDE VIEW

CREATE A NATURAL LOOKING OUTCROP

No matter how individual pieces are positioned, they must relate to each other as though representing bedrock exposed by natural weathering or as a result of gulleying by water or wind. This means the major rock faces will have the same general direction throughout the garden, and if the stone shows lines of stratification they will be at the same angle throughout. Minor exceptions are when rocks represent pieces broken away from the main body and that angle downward from the cliff-like margins of a gullied stream or have tumbled from a cliff to repose on a slope or plateau below. Fairly small rocks may be effectively employed to give the impression of being a bold outcrop.

Although it is true that natural outcrops occur in which, as a result of geological upheavals, their lines of stratification run vertically or nearly so, and there are others in which they are approximately horizontal, it is much easier and generally makes for the most satisfactory accommodation of a considerable variety of plants if in constructed rock gardens they are established at an angle of from ten to forty degrees from the horizontal. This means of course that the joints between the long sides of adjacent stones will run similarly, which emphasizes the stratification.

In natural formations of stratified rock, fractures, called primary joints, spaced from one foot or so to up to about five feet apart, commonly occur along the sides of uptilted masses, but not along their faces. These are at right angles to the lines of stratification and cleave the rock into approximately rectangular blocks. They may be simulated in constructed rock gardens by positioning the ends of individual stones to produce chinks and crevices that cross the lines of stratification at right angles and where exposed surfaces, which consist of superimposed pieces of rock, extend through more than one layer. To accomplish this, take care not to place the rocks like bricks in a wall with their vertical separations staggered, but have them above one another, with the chinks thus formed angling downward from the tilted top of the exposed rock.

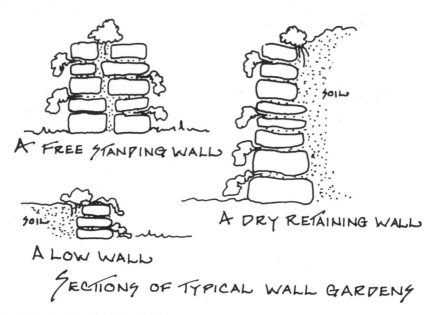

A FREE STANDING WALL

A DRY RETAINING WALL

A LOW WALL

SECTIONS OF TYPICAL WALL GARDENS

The ends of uplifted masses of stratified rock show no regular system of primary joints, such as just described, but they may be creviced vertically by frost action or as a result of water running down them.

Whether the garden be big or whether it occupies no more space than an average living room, the principles discussed are applicable. Only scale differs. In large gardens, bolder features necessitating the use of larger rocks are needed, and by the same token, rockless or sparingly rocked portions can be more expansive.

The final effect must be one of rightness, of belonging. If the development adjoins a house or other building, make sure it seems that the rock is native and the structure was built upon it, rather than rocks have been brought in and piled or positioned against or in front of the building. And if your rock garden is to outcrop from a lawn or meadow, perhaps rising no more than a couple of feet or so above ground level, perhaps higher, let it, by the way it slopes into the ground, suggest firm ties with imaginary underlying bedrock.

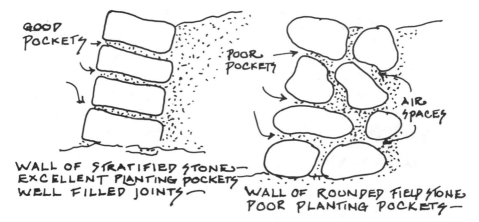

GOOD POCKETS

POOR POCKETS

AIR SPACES

WALL OF STRATIFIED STONE—
EXCELLENT PLANTING POCKETS
WELL FILLED JOINTS—

WALL OF ROUNDED FIELD STONE
POOR PLANTING POCKETS—

Scree and Moraine

A scree or moraine is often included as part of a rock garden. Such developments are patterned after natural features of the same names that occur in mountain regions. Their special characteristic depends upon the material of which they are formed and into which the plants root. This mostly consists of fragmented rock, in natural screes detritus collected in rock slides and at the bases of cliffs, and in moraines along the fronts and sides of glaciers. Natural moraines are further commonly characterized by having flowing through them some distance below the surface cold melt water from the ice. It is less natural for screes to have any constant flow beneath the surface.

Rock garden screes and moraines simulate to a degree natural ones. Their purpose is to provide plants with extremely well-aerated rooting mixes of low fertility. Surface water should drain through them rapidly, leaving a film around each particle to meet the needs of the plants.

RAIN

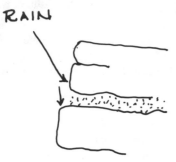

RAIN

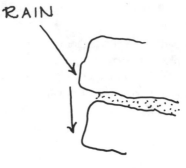

GOOD

POOR

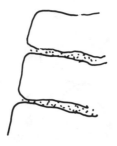

RIGHT
BACKWARD PITCH

WRONG
FORWARD PITCH

STONE WEDGE USED TO HOLD
PLANT SECURELY IN PLACE

PLANTING POCKETS

Portion of the Colorado Garden of Dick & Ann Bartlett. *Photo by Dick Bartlett.*

John & Mary Jim English Garden, Salt Lake City. *Photo by John English.*

Handmade rocks and pool in Harland Hand California garden. *Photo by Pamela Harper.*

Marcia Tatroe flagstone garden in late summer. *Photo by Randy Tatroe.*

Leonard Buck New Jersey garden, designed by Zenon Schreiber. *Photo by Paul Halladin.*

Phyllis Gustafson's Czech crevice garden in Oregon. *Photo by Phyllis Gustafson.*

A Rock Garden Handbook for Beginners

To make a scree, which may well slope away from the base of a cliff-like rock or occupy a sloping gulley, install over a base of crushed stone or other very adequate drainage a foot or more of a mix consisting very largely of crushed stone or gravel, grit, and coarse sand with a small admixture of topsoil. Approximate proportions may well be one half by bulk crushed stone or gravel, and one quarter part each grit or sand and soil, but these proportions may be varied somewhat depending upon the character of ingredients.

A moraine, in the horticultural sense, differs from a scree, although the words are often used interchangeably, in that a foot or two below its surface there is a constant slow flow of water. This may be arranged by a shallow basin of concrete or one formed of clay or of earth covered with heavy polyethylene film as a base, with faucet or other source of a trickle of water supplying one end and an outlet at the other. To be most harmonious, arrange for the surface of the scree or moraine to slope gently away from the base of a cliff or down a gulley and have a few pieces of rock a little bigger than the average, of which the rooting mix largely consists, showing at the surface.

Planting the Garden

Planting a newly-built rock garden is best, but not necessarily, delayed for a few weeks to allow for any settling of the soil or rocks that may occur. But if each rock is set on a firm base and the soil is packed well around it and between neighbor rocks there will be little, if any, movement, and planting may begin as soon as convenient. Early spring and early fall are the most propitious seasons for this work.

When placing the plants keep two objectives in mind: any special needs of individual kinds and the overall effect you are creating. If the first is not respected, as for instance the need of dianthus for exposure to sun, of primulas for some shade, of ramondas for a vertical crevice, of sorts finicky about the pH of the soil for acid or alkaline areas, and of other kinds for drier or moister soils, the growth, the flowering, and even the permanence of the plants may be adversely affected.

Endeavor to achieve a relaxed landscape, a feeling of naturalness. If too many single plants of different kinds are spotted around, or if there are not some areas, fair-sized in relation to the extent of the garden, clothed with low creepers such as thymes, creeping phloxes, or *Mazus* to afford rest for the eye, the effect will be too busy. If groups of the same kind are too equal in size, are of too formal an outline, or are of individuals too evenly spaced, the effect will be unnatural.

Some single specimens advantageously located may serve as special points of interest. Especially appropriate for such use are selected varieties of dwarf conifers, among them arborvitaes, cedars, false cypresses, firs, hemlocks, junipers, pines, and spruces. Occasional individuals of other kinds of plants may be used similarly.

But for the most part, plant in informal groups and drifts that suggest a natural ecological association of kinds. This requires knowledge about how different sorts will grow after planting. You may have this information. If not, acquire as much as you can by observing other gardens and by reading.

Groups may drift down gentle slopes, with the plants closer together in the upper than the lower end of the group and with perhaps a few specimens irregularly placed some little distance from the low side of the main planting. Such outliers suggest the results of seeds dropped or washed from a higher place.

Other groups may occupy little plateaus, hang from the tops of cliffs, or below crevices. They need not be clearly defined. If adjacent groups mingle somewhat at their margins, and if an occasional plant of one crops up as it were as a seedling inside a group of another kind, the effect of naturalness is enhanced.

No matter how knowledgeable and careful you are, it is not improbable that some errors of judgment will creep into your selection of spots for some plants, but if these be comparatively few they can be corrected later by transplanting to sites that afford better growing conditions or more appropriate display.

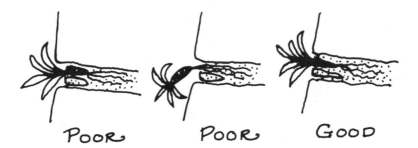

POOR   POOR   GOOD

CROWN TOO DEEP   CROWN EXPOSED

INSERTING PLANTS IN POCKETS

Choose time for planting when the soil is pleasantly damp, neither wet nor dust dry. Make sure the roots of plants dug in readiness for planting are protected from exposure to sun and wind. Space individuals with some regard for the amount of top growth they are expected to make. Do not break the balls of soil in which roots are growing, but spread roots not encased in soil in their natural positions and work soil between them. Set the plants at the same depths or very slightly deeper than they were previously, firm the soil around them, and soak with a fine spray of water.

Mulch
Depending upon the kind of plant and the part of the rock garden it is to occupy, the surface between individual plants may be mulched lightly with chips or fragments of stone or, about woodland plants in shaded areas, with screened leaf mold or peat moss mixed with grit or coarse sand. For the best effect, see that the stone chips consist of a mixture of sizes and are of the same or closely matching kind of rock to that of which the garden is constructed.

Care of the Garden

Routine care of the rock garden demands regular attention, but not arduous toil. Beginning in the late winter or early spring, the first task in regions of cold winters without an adequate blanket of snow is the removal of the winter covering. Do this before growth is well advanced and in two or three stages rather than all at one time, so that new shoots and foliage become gradually accustomed to full exposure.

Choose dull, humid, quiet days rather than sunny, windy ones for taking off the cover. Push back into place any plants that have been heaved up by frost action and replace any labels that have been disturbed.

Do not be in too great haste to cut back what appears to be the lifeless tops of woody-stemmed plants. Some may surprise you by leafing later. But if you are certain they are dead, do not hesitate, and at the same time clear away dead foliage and any weeds overlooked from the previous year.

Topdressing is next. Prepare a porous mix of topsoil, peat moss and grit or coarse sand as a base and modify it as needed for particular areas of the garden devoted to plants with special needs by adding additional peat moss for acid soil plants, crushed limestone or agricultural lime for lovers of alkaline soils, bonemeal for plants likely to benefit from some extra nutrients, and for kinds known to appreciate richer diets, such as primulas, some old rotted or dried commercial cow manure. But beware of using too much fertilizer. The vast majority of rock garden plants thrive in rather lean soils and become too lush and gross in those too fertile. Before spreading the topdressing, stir the soil shallowly with a hand cultivator so that the new layer will integrate with the old.

Summer care consists chiefly of weeding, watering (do this only when clearly needed and then soak the ground to a depth of several inches), and taking off faded flowers, plus a certain amount of propagation. Weeding calls for special knowledge. In a garden containing many species and varieties it is not a job for a novice or an oddjob man. Not infrequently, choice plants that perhaps have defied the gardener's best efforts to propagate reproduce voluntarily and one or more precious seedlings will appear in some unlikely spot, in a crevice, on a little plateau, or perhaps among some spreading plant of another kind. Only the keen eye of an experienced rock gardener is likely to detect such dividends, with the result that instead of being ruthlessly rooted out they are nurtured to add yet further glory to the garden. Besides, weeding in a rock garden can be a delightful task, one that gives opportunity to know one's plants more intimately, to observe their manners of growth, and to note their individual idiosyncrasies, that is, if weeding is done when it should be, at the very earliest evidence of the weed growth and before it has begun to take over from the rightful occupants.

In the fall a general cleanup is needed. Cut back the dead tops of plants that are not evergreen and make comfortable for the winter all that are perennial. This is the time, too, to plant hardy spring-flowering bulbs.

Winter protection in regions where hard freezing is experienced, but a continuous snow cover cannot be relied upon, is necessary, but it is easy to overdo this. Do not install the cover until the ground is frozen to a depth of 2 or 3 inches, otherwise mice and other rodents may establish winter quarters and harm plants. A covering of branches of evergreens (discarded

Christmas trees are fine for this purpose) such as pines, spruces, or hemlocks, is ideal. Or salt hay can be used. It is important that air circulates freely through the covering. Common errors are to put in place too early and too thickly.

Propagating the Plants

Propagation is an important phase of rock gardening. Many of the very finest rock plants are comparatively short-lived or are fickle in cultivation. This makes it necessary always to have at hand a stock of young plants to replace those that may succumb to the heat and humidity of the summer, to the extreme conditions of winter, or to other causes. Raising young plants is fascinating work and makes a particular appeal to the real plant lover.

Rock garden plants are increased in several ways, and the method followed in any particular case will depend upon the character of the plant, the availability of propagating material, and the percentage of increase desired.

Plants of a mat-forming type, such as creeping thymes, *Mazus*, and *Draba repens*, are easily increased by simple division of old sods. This method also serves splendidly for many kinds that form clumps, as do most veronicas, primulas, and asters. If more rapid increase is desired, or if divisions are not obtainable, cuttings afford an alternative method of securing additional stock. Seed provides an excellent means of obtaining stock of many wild species of plants, but it is not reliable for garden varieties or for improved kinds that you may want to grow. Then again, the species of certain genera hybridize very freely if they are grown near to one another, thus seed collected from any such species growing in a garden where others of the same genus are grown will very likely result in hybrid progeny of unpredictable characteristics and desirability. Dianthus, aquilegias, saxifrages, and sempervivums are typical of this group.

Many rock garden plants can be propagated in the spring. September is also an excellent time to attend to this work, for at this season the trying conditions that have prevailed during July and August no longer have to be faced, and the young plants still have an opportunity to become established before the onset of winter. Stock of kinds known or suspected not to be reliably hardy must be established in pots and plunged to the rims of the pots in a bed of sand in a cold frame for the duration of the winter.

Division is, of course, the simplest means of propagation. All that is necessary is to lift the parent plant and carefully divide it into suitably-sized portions, each with some roots attached. If the plant has a great deal of top growth, this is usually cut back somewhat to compensate for the unavoidable root disturbance caused by the operation. The divisions are then planted directly back into the rock garden or potted into the smallest size pot into which their roots can be comfortably fitted in a soil mixture similar to, but lighter than that in which established plants of the same kind are known to thrive. The addition to the soil mixture of a liberal amount of grit or coarse sand ensures lightness. Shade from strong sunlight must be provided, at least until new roots have thoroughly taken possession of the medium in which divisions are growing.

A cutting is essentially a division without roots that, if placed in an appropriate environment, may be expected to develop a new root system. Until new roots are sent out, cuttings require special care, and every effort must be made to provide conditions favorable to root development. The medium in which cuttings are planted is usually clean, coarse sand or perlite kept constantly and evenly moist, but some kinds, for instance heaths and heathers, root more readily in a mixture of sand or perlite and peat moss. Protection from currents of moving air, shade from direct sunshine, and the maintenance of humid atmosphere check excessive transpiration and evaporation. This is important because if the cutting continues to lose from its tissues more moisture than it is able to replace, it quickly withers and dies. A well-managed cold frame provides suitable conditions for rooting cuttings of a great many rock garden plants. If a considerable number are to be inserted, install a three to four inch deep bed of the rooting medium in the frame. For lesser quantities, a flat will suffice. Be sure that the medium is moist and packed down firmly by pounding it with a brick or an equivalent tool.

The cuttings will vary in length according to kind, the smallest perhaps not exceeding one half inch, the largest up to three inches. Cut them cleanly across with a keen knife or razor blade at the base just below a joint or node, and trim off the lower leaves. Plant them so the base of each sits squarely on the bottom of the hole it occupies, and pack the sand firmly against it. After the cuttings are planted, water them thoroughly with a fine spray, and then cover the frame with the sash. In the beginning, ventilate not at all or at most sparingly and provide shade from direct sunshine. But when the cuttings commence to form roots, more ventilation and less shade are in order and finally the young plants should be exposed to the ordinary outdoor conditions that suit their kind.

As soon as good root systems have developed, transplant the new plants into small pots. Use a gritty or sandy soil mix and make sure of good drainage by putting into the bottom of each pot a few crocks. After potting, sink the plants to the rim of their pots in sand or peat moss in a cold frame.

Plants from Seed

Raising alpine or other rock garden plants from seed sometimes brings interesting problems, but it is impossible to generalize as to procedures except in the broadest way. Experience and observation suggest that the importance of compounding exact soil mixes to meet the requirements of individual species is frequently overstressed. In their early stages at least, the vast majority of plants can be successfully raised in one of three distinct types of soil. The first contains lime, preferably in the form of ground limestone, but ordinary builders lime will do. The second is free of lime, but contains an abundance of leaf mold or peat moss. The latter is particularly desirable for plants known to need an acid soil. The third is an ordinary, porous seed soil, such as you would use for the majority of garden annuals, but considerably more gritty. This type will be used most often, since the majority of plants thrive in it during their early stages. Lime-loving plants such as encrusted saxifrages, need the first mixture. Woodland plants in general prefer the second mix. Of far more importance for most sorts than the exact chemical reaction of the soil is its physical condition. It must be porous and drain freely.

Pots, pans, or flats, according to the amount of seed to be sown, may be used. Most gardeners agree that it is desirable, after sowing, to expose the seeds of alpine plants to freezing or near-freezing temperatures for a few weeks before putting them into a cool greenhouse or similar environment to germinate. But often the most practical plan is to sow seeds as soon as they are obtainable. Many will germinate in a few days to a few weeks, others may take several months, even a year or longer. Keep moist those that do not germinate quickly, and in fall sink their containers to their rims in a bed of sand or peat moss in a cold frame or outdoors. They may be left there until they germinate, or to hasten germination, they may be brought into a cool greenhouse in February. Alternatively, mix the seeds with slightly damp sand or peat moss and store them in a plastic bag in a refrigerator at 35 to 40°F for three or four months before sowing.

Detailed care following germination plays an important part in the degree of success attained. It is particularly important that the soil be kept uniformly moist. When the seedlings are of such size that they can be transplanted, a little more thought than when seed sowing should be given to the exact soil mix most suitable for each particular kind. Only by experience and experiment, and often a certain amount of error, can these facts be determined, for above all, it is unwise to be too dogmatic about a subject having such wide ramifications as this. Frequently, gardeners following widely different practices get equally good results provided fundamental principles are not violated.

Rock garden plants for temperate and cold temperate climates include a vast array of alpines as well as natives of lower elevations that, by custom and for convenience, are accepted as appropriate. Most are species and varieties that somewhere occur as wildlings, but practically all rock gardeners admit a selection of garden varieties and man-made hybrids. These are usually limited to sorts that look as if they could be natural species and varieties, although this is scarcely true of a few that have double flowers. Nevertheless, it is generally considered inappropriate to admit plants of distinctly gardenesque appearance, those that strongly suggest the hand of the plant breeder.

A founding member of the North American Rock Garden Society in 1934, Thomas H. Everett was the author of the mammoth 1980-1981 ten-volume New York Botanical Garden Illustrated Encyclopedia of Horticulture.

A New Garden: Starting from Scratch

by Gwen Kelaidis

A new garden is like a blank canvas. Anything is possible, and everything depends on you. When we moved to a new property in October of 1994, I was both excited and a bit intimidated. Now I have half an acre, whereas before we had a 52' by 100' lot (with a house and garage taking up way too much space). By my rough calculations the growing area (all the land not covered by buildings) is six times as great here.

Much of my gardening in the last eight years had been influenced - or should I say determined - by the small scale in which I gardened. I have been a fanatic advocate of small plants. After all, the smaller the plants, the more I could jam into that space. No plant which flopped or spread rapidly was allowed to live there: too dangerous to its cohabitors, too greedy, and out of proportion to the compact size of the many cushion plants I grew. But now all assumptions were brought into question, and it was a new world of gardening.

When starting fresh on a new garden, many questions arise. If you are beginning a new garden, or viewing your yard from an altered perspective with the idea of rearranging, here are some questions to consider:

Are there trees, shrubs, and structures of the existing landscaping that should be removed?

Many times there are trees or shrubs that have no particular merit, and you want to replace them either with sun-loving perennials or with a choice woody plant. Also, most rock plants prefer sun. If you have trees, you may wish to thin them even if you are growing primarily woodlanders.

In my case, it was obvious that about 30 junipers were to be removed. A blue spruce grew in the middle of the area I anticipated as a future rock garden, so it became a Christmas tree. Sacrifices to snobbery and re-shaping the garden spaces included a spirea, a Russian Olive, a Peking cotoneaster at the corner of the sunporch, and a privet. I have evil intentions towards the silver maple, but it provides nice shade for the side yard, and before I remove it I'll underplant it.

Where should the rockgarden(s) be?

Consider your view of the rock garden. Will you be able to view it from the house or deck? How much light will it receive? For me, there are to be several rock gardens, some shady, others bright and well-watered, another bright and dry. Actually, at least half of the yard is planned for rock garden.

Does the overall grade of the yard need to be changed?

Whether your site is on a hill or a flat piece of land, consider major grading changes before you put the rock garden in place. Unlike the perennial border, there is much labor involved in the construction of a rock garden. It's much easier to abandon even double digging than it is to move those rocks, once in place. Here we are on a hill with over 15' of drop from the top of the lot to the bottom. When we moved in, there were a series of terraces. I plan to have at least three parallel ridges from top to bottom. I graded the top corner behind the house largely by hand, since it is inaccessible and since I wanted quite a bit of detail.

Remember to make sure that the grade slopes away from the buildings.

Do supporting structures need to be built before the rock garden goes in?
If a rock garden is to be bordered by a fence or a wall, it is usually best to build that first.

Where will the paths be, especially to the doors and to gates?
Before you start the rock garden, try to figure out which paths will automatically be taken by the dogs, the paperboy, and the mailman. Either block these paths with emphatic rock work or cede to them and design around them. Also, if you want a meandering feel to the garden or want to create a series of garden rooms, plan these out before you set the first rock.

Speaking of setting the first rock, this is a great moment, which should be celebrated with champagne-or at least a drink of cool water. The first rock often sets the direction and the tone and will influence the placement of other rocks, whether you intend it to or not. Don't let yourself be rushed in this decision. Be sure that you like it before going on. I have often moved this rock five times before going on.

Where will the utility area (frames, gravel, soil stores) be located?
Choose now, rather than after the fact. You'll need access to extra materials throughout the life of the garden.

What about soil?
I still consider soil a mystery. Who really measures out one-third of this, one - third of that? I add sand, gravel, manure, leaf-mold, whatever I can get my hands on, whatever looks "right," until I have a loose, good-looking texture. It's not scientific – or I am not!

What kind of rock will you use?
This is always a hot topic. The classic rock garden preference is for stratified rock. Weathered limestone is my very favorite. It's easy to arrange in credible-looking outcrops or ridges; it is attractive in its own right; it holds quite a bit of water on the surface, many plants like it; etc. I saw some beautiful rocks of this sort last year but didn't have the funds to invest. Now that particular rock yard doesn't have that particular rock any more. Well, choose rock that is available and affordable for you. Sometimes this involves making an arrangement with a landowner to pick rocks out of the fields yourself. In some areas of the country, like Denver, we have the luxury of many sand and materials companies that sell rock. After a while, it seems worthwhile to have someone else load the truck. Also, I have personally broken more than one set of truck springs. Delivery is expensive, but trucks are, too.

Most important of all is to get rock that pleases you personally. I have ended by choosing granite for at least one section of this garden. Choose rock for which you can find a matching gravel mulch. Sometimes large, beautiful cap rocks, formed by much weathering at the surface, have no accompanying gravel mulch available. All the gravel that size weathered away many eons ago!

Some prefer large rocks hoisted into place by cranes. Landscape designers are often inclined to recommend these, perhaps suggesting that they are more in scale with the house. I like smaller rocks, ones that I can move around by myself or with one other person. Selling large rocks is obviously more profitable than selling small rocks, since you pay by the ton. Keep looking until you find what you want.

Another note of caution: it is well to obtain about a third more rocks than you think you will need. No matter how many rocks you have, you always want a different one for that spot you are working on.

What will you plant?

Now for the fun! Once again, let your own personal tastes lead you in your choices. The first thing to consider is which plants are adapted to your conditions. You need to know how much shade each area receives, how much water there is, what your soil type is. In this   garden I have extremely sandy soil, modified by considerable quantities of leaf mold and cow manure. I have always had a base soil of clay loam in the past, modified with manure, sand, and gravel. Some plants simply don't care for sand, while others adore it, and I am sure I will kill many plants along the way to developing a list of what does well here.

In practice, I try to have a site for every kind of plant. So far, I've only managed to provide a shady garden under pines. My latest plans include everything from bog to dryland.

The charm of having a wide range of habitats, is that you can then buy whatever plants are attractive to you, and that will no doubt include many, many, many plants. What you read about and can't find commercially available you can grow. What you can't grow you can trade for with other gardeners. There's nothing to be ashamed of in occasional begging, by the way. There are not a few plants after which we have lusted for 20 years. Many come to you eventually, as to Penelope. Others remain the inspiration for continued searching and communication with fellow gardeners, more like the Holy Grail. When planting, remember that the soil will be moister at the base of a slope than at the top, just as a sponge set on end will be wetter at the bottom. Also, the north slope has quite a bit colder conditions than the south side. If you are not sure where to plant something, buy two or three and try it in   different exposures. If you kill just one plant, you learn little; if one lives and two die, you have had the opportunity to learned something.

When will construction begin?

Why now, of course! Isn't it summer? If it's raining, think of West Texas, be grateful, and start tomorrow!

Gwen Kelaidis has been starting new gardens since 1976. She claims this is her magnum opus and has enough planned to keep her busy for at least 25 years. She gardens with her husband and children very near Denver, Colorado.

Do As I Say—Not As I Do:
Eighteen Commandments for a Rock Garden

by G. K. Fenderson

1.   The garden should remain as open and uncluttered as possible, with a minimum number of visual distractions. It is neither necessary nor desirable that all of it should be visible at once; rather those areas which are visible should present a unified, well thought-out picture with balance, interest, perspective, and, above all, restraint. A natural visual progression from one area of the garden to another should be apparent. Not every plant in the collection should be on display at once. An ideal garden would consist of a gradually unfolding series of plant tableaus, each constructed with the intent of providing an ideal cultural and aesthetic setting for its components.

2.   Be bold with the initial layout of the garden. Make sure that paths are adequate for wheelbarrows, mowers, garden tractors, and pedestrians. Generosity in the size of the planting area to be developed will help eliminate crowding and clutter if your garden is small and will provide ease of access for maintenance.

3.   Be bold with the use of rocks; use but few, use them strategically, and make sure they are large and significant enough to be in scale with the remainder of the planting. Make sure they appear settled and are of a color and texture not alien to the raw materials of the garden. If they are none of these things, do not use them.

4.   Leave some uninterrupted vista, be it water, lawn, rough meadow, uncluttered woodland glade, or distant prospect, to rest the eye. Visual breathing space is important.

5.   When planting gardens under or near trees, be extremely critical of which trees (and of which species) you retain. Removing natural visual clutter often can produce better design than any number of additions you might make. Trees to be eliminated should be selected well in advance of developing the rock garden. Strive to have your site appear as attractive as possible before any plantings are made. Remember, the site will remain the permanent showcase of your collections.

6.   Don't overplant. Allow space for plants to grow and develop uncrowded to their best advantage. Don't shortchange yourself of future pleasure by opting for instant garden effect; such efforts are costly, extremely short-lived, and can mean much extra work and the loss of valuable plants within a short time.

7.   Be bold with the use of accent plants—those with distinctive form, color, or texture. But use them in extreme moderation; otherwise that which makes them distinctive is lost in a clamor of many contrasts.

8.   Choose for the backbone or focal points of your design only plants of known durability, hardiness, general good health, and long season of interest. Leave for the background or less conspicuous areas plants of marginal hardiness, those that are prone to pests, those that have a shabby dormancy, and those of mere botanical interest however rare.

9.   Enliven the monotonous effect of collections of closely-allied plants by including plants dramatically different in form and texture.

10.   Give full consideration to heights, lengths, and general proportions of planting areas. For example, a stiffly rectangular raised bed, though perhaps easier to build, would be visually jarring in a garden where the majority of the line were soft curves. So too would a very free-form simulated rock outcropping in a very formal surroundings.

11.   Keep the use of man-made and non-indigenous materials (such as cement, brick, slate, railroad ties, newly quarried or foreign stone, glass, and plastic) to a minimum. Do not mix mediums unnecessarily. For example, if there is a need for a raised bed, try to incorporate it into an existing wall or structure. Build it with native stone whenever possible, rather than contrast the fieldstone of one bed with the bricks of another and the wooden ties of yet another.

12.   Be conscious of surface texture and try to avoid too many varieties and discordant combinations. For example, a rock garden mulched with very light or highly colored stone in a woodland setting appears unnatural, however beneficial the topdressing may be to the plants being grown there. Likewise a mulch of pine needles looks strikingly out of place in an open sunny area far removed from any pine trees. Use native mulches whenever they would be less distracting to the eye. They are usually cheaper and more readily available.

13.   Provide a generous cold frame and nursery area. Such an area, used for propagation and evaluation of plants before they earn a place in the landscape, will contribute greatly to the overall appearance and order of a garden.

14.   Try to have a yearly housecleaning. Give excess plants away or discard them. Remain constantly conscious as to whether a specific plant is justified in terms of the space and time required for its care. Be critical of inferior clones; grow only the best. Try to avoid redundant collections. Don't allow your garden to resemble either a warehouse of plants or a hospital ward of perpetual invalids.

15.   Try to rebuild and correct defects in old gardens before developing new areas.

16.   Label only the most recent acquisitions and those of which you are uncertain. Labels are often an intrusion in the landscape, and their lack improves the memory. If you must collect, collect plants, not labels. Don't allow your garden to resemble a cemetery for mice.

17.   Invite the NARGS frequently. This will improve your housekeeping.

18.   Know when to leave well enough alone. Have the self-discipline not to intrude too much into the natural landscape.

G. Kris Fenderson is a New Hampshire gardener with a special interest in primroses. He is the author of A Synoptic Guide to the Genus *Primula (1986).*

Construction of a Rock Garden

by Karl H. Grieshaber

The form and style we select for the rock garden and the way it is actually constructed will depend in part on the inclination and physical ability of the person who will cultivate the garden. The form and style may also, in part, depend on the natural features of the location and the building materials available locally.

We will discuss applications of the many principles we have examined and see how those which have proved practical and successful may be used in building rock gardens. After all, a garden is not nature, but a work of art, something artificially created which merely makes use of natural means to form a different but always harmonic picture. A rock garden is always a work of art just because in it nature is outwitted and plants are made to grow in places where under normal circumstances they might grow only very sparsely or not at all. We want to attain in a rock garden visual effects which nature would never venture on its own.

Visualizing the Effect

This is the first and most fundamental consideration in the construction. The landscape architect, a master of materials, always keeps in mind the plants' value to the composition at maturity. The amateur, without this knowledge, often becomes bewildered by the very abundance from which to choose. He decides in desperation that one thing will do as well as another.

To this same principle belongs the choice of style most suitable to the locality and the proper scale of the design when applied to the ground. The interrelation of mass, texture, form, color, and detail is the product of the rock gardener's degree of adherence to the principle of composition. The garden must relate to the human scale—no miniature Matterhorns. We have to reduce the overpowering size of the universe and bring it down to cozier proportions in a small private world. A rock garden must have a definite unity of design with both esthetic and utilitarian functions.

Siting the Garden

The particular effect to be developed in a rock garden depends largely upon the portion of the property that is used. Quite often the first choice for a rock garden is that part not needed for anything else, or the one that has proven difficult to tie into the general design of the total landscape. This is not always the best spot.

Generally speaking, most rock gardens can be classified under formal and informal or naturalistic. With that in mind we must visualize which kind will fit best into the existing landscape. The formal style is usually best close to the house, sometimes in the form of terraced walls, raised beds, or as wide steps with enough open space for plants.

Observe the exposure of the sun at different parts of the day on various portions of the property. A southern exposure ensures the maximum amount of sunlight to sun-loving plants; however it also exposes them to prolonged summer heat and to the injurious effects of

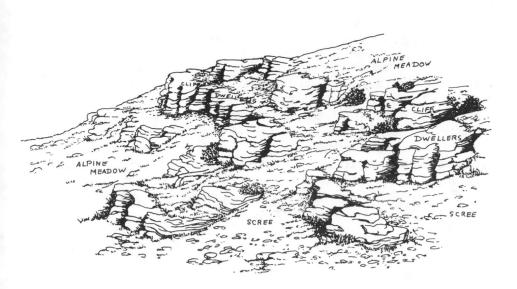

Rock garden constructed on a slope with weathered limestone rocks.

alternate freezing and thawing in winter. A northern or even an eastern exposure is generally preferable for plant growth. Consider also the prevailing wind direction.

Avoid a site which cannot be properly drained. Bear in mind that though alpines grow under widely differing aspects and conditions, they do not tolerate sour, badly drained soil. Neither will they do well when exposed to drought and cutting winds. Do not build a rock garden for alpines under overhanging branches of trees or between buildings where drafts and shade will discomfort the plants growing there.

A factor which may indirectly affect the choice of a location is the provision of water for pool and streams. Only in a few gardens is natural water found. So if this feature is desired, it must usually be introduced artificially. A rock garden doesn't necessarily need a watercourse, but water surely enhances its character.

In selecting a spot for the future rock garden, there is one point which may seem of secondary importance but is really quite essential. That is having easy access for the bulky and often heavy material and equipment that will be required. Disregarding this point could add considerably to the cost of construction, to say nothing of damage done to lawns and other parts of the garden.

No work should be started before a suitable position has been selected and it has been decided from which direction the garden is most likely to be viewed. Foreground and background are part of the composition and have to be considered. Objects of a distracting nature should be eliminated or concealed to prevent the eye from straying away from the

33

garden itself. The immediate foreground of a hillside planting should be part of the design. Here is a perfect place for an alpine lawn with stepping stones set among the plants for easy access to the rock outcropping at the rear.

The Stone Material

In constructing a naturalistic rock garden the aim is to select and arrange rocks in such a manner that each appears as a natural deposit which has not been disturbed by man. A rock garden should not be a meaningless jumble of rocks showing drill marks and glaring or newly exposed surfaces, nor should the rocks be set up in unnatural and unstable positions. The best stone for use in the rock garden is that of local origin. The porousness of the stone is a factor of considerable importance because the stone stores moisture and is always cool underground. Alpine plants like a situation where they can press their roots as close as possible to the side of a rock. In this respect, the sandstones and limestones are the best material for rock gardens. Granite may also be used but is hard and gives an acid reaction to the soil. Quartz is too hard and too conspicuous.

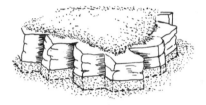

1. The first planting pocket is completed. The rocks have only one-third to one-fourth of their heights in the ground and each one is slightly overlapping the rock behind.

2. Beginning of the next elevation. The corner rock touches the rock below.

3. The baseline of the next elevation forms a somewhat triangular planting pocket in the lower bed.

4. The procession of stepped planting pockets can be continued indefinitely.

A Rock Garden Handbook for Beginners

As a rule, unstratified stone such as granite, trap, glacial boulders, and conglomerate all weather in round forms. These boulders can never be made into a stratified outcropping: their place is on a rugged boulder-strewn slope, some scattered, others in dense steep clusters. On a rather steep slope, the rock should give the effect of a stream-cut bank where the softer material has been eroded away to expose the outcropping boulders. Stream valleys and pond areas are excellent locations for such arrangements of rock. The size of the rocks used should be determined by the scale of the garden. Large rocks give the effect of strength, but a big boulder in a small garden makes the area seem smaller. Too many small rocks give an artificial and weak effect. Only weathered boulders should be selected, and these should be embedded in the soil to their weathered line or their widest circumference.

Another good way to use unmatched rounded stone is a moraine. Millennia ago, glaciers transported erratic blocks from a distance. The action of frost, rain, and wind changed the surface of granite, feldspar, and porphyry blocks so that everything on them is round, smoothed off, and dome-shaped. No one block matches the others.

The individual character of each rock must be considered when constructing a moraine. Erratic blocks cannot be used in the same way as matching stratified or sedimentary stone. They must be embedded in the soil as if they had been resting there unmoved since the glacier left them stranded. To do this is not an easy task. The individual rocks should all face a common main direction. If the moraine is resting against a stone wall in a small garden, then the main direction should be parallel to the wall. The joints between the rocks should be diagonal to the main direction. Or a rock garden of such blocks may be built on a gentle mound evenly sloped from side to side. Here the largest rock should dominate. The surface of the rocks must all be given the same inclined plane to the lowest point. This order in the direction is an architectonic device to avoid confusion.

When building with stratified stones such as limestone and sandstone, it is necessary to understand its stratification and jointing to obtain a natural effect. The lines of stratification are traceable throughout the entire formation. In the garden it does not matter at what angle the strata are inclined so long as this angle is kept throughout. A backward tilt has the advantage of holding some of the rainfall and conducting it into the soil. With some ingenuity it is possible with this kind of stone to provide a variety of crevices and planting spots, some in full sun, others where it is cool and shaded behind a bend or larger rock.

A limestone or sandstone formation is suitable for most informal garden effects. Where this type of stone occurs naturally, it would be difficult to find better or easier material for the garden, especially if it is porous, irregular in form, and already weathered to a rather neutral color. Avoid sandstones which disintegrate easily and limestones which crumble away because of atmospheric action.

Hillocks and Stone Knolls

The remains of many old artificial hillocks, planted with alpines, can still be seen in botanical gardens in Europe. Even today many collectors of alpine plants insist that this is the most practical construction for growing and displaying plants that are all native of the same habitat. This is especially important for gardens and institutions which consider it their obligation to educate the public and stimulate interest in wild plants. To do this, public and botanical gardens often find it most practical to arrange stony hillocks to correspond to the mountainous areas of a continent or the mountain ranges of a country. Alpine plants can then be distributed on the hillocks representing the mountains of their native habitat. Moreover, this method of display presents an opportunity to select for the individual knolls the kind of stone that corresponds to the terrain of the mountains being represented. Thus the layout offers all at the same time an orographic, geognostic, and phytogeographic picture of a mountain or district to the student and lover of alpines. For all their good points, however, the knolls or hillocks will always look somewhat artificial.

Terraced rock garden against a wall.

Depending on the form and space available and the goals for growing alpines, some modifications are necessary if this concept is to be tried in the home garden. If the space for the rock garden happens to be along a low wall or the face of a cliff or on the side of an excavated bank of soil, it would be suitable to pile the rocks up to form an elongated terrace running parallel to the wall or cliff or bank and rising like stairs up to the top.

On the other hand, hillocks that are free standing and constructed as modified terraced pyramids have the advantage of being conveniently accessible from all sides and presenting a multitude of suitable planting exposures for a wider variety of plants. As a rule, it is better to build several stone knolls close together, each with steep sides, rather that a single mountain of boulders. This makes it easy to walk around each hillock to care for and examine the plants.. It also means that the plants are less exposed to drying winds in winter and that drifting snow may fill the hollows between the knolls. These snow-filled depressions resemble the little snow valleys we find in the mountains where snow remains even into early summer. This is precisely what we try to accomplish, to prolong the rest period as far into spring as possible.

The traditional hillocks had a height of not more than six feet and a base not more than four feet in diameter. These towering stone knolls provided enough crevices for cliff dwellers, gave maximum drainage, and raised the plants close to the eye level of the observer. The

The old-fashioned stone knolls are ideal for growing plants but will always look artificial.

visitor stood in the garden, surrounded on all sides by an alpine environment, rather than looking from outside at the garden which faced in only one direction. In addition, most of these hillocks had a built-in mist or sprinkler system which could be turned on to simulate the clouds and fog of the mountains, thus keeping the plants cool and moist in hot, dry weather.

The construction of the individual stone knolls and the way in which they are interrelated is important. A knoll should never give the appearance of a piece of dry wall, nor should the rocks be scattered carelessly on top of a soil mound. We strive for the natural effect of erosion caused by water and wind rather than a man-made construction. Such a garden, of course, will look more natural when built on a slope, or even better, on two opposite slopes with a small stream running between them. If done skillfully, however, level ground will do as well. In that case, the construction should be designed more or less as a sunken garden with the excavated soil piled at the top of the sides.

In building these knolls it is important that the lower layers and interiors be made of material through which excess water can trickle and drain. Broken rocks of all sizes, fragments of brick, and sand should be alternated with peat moss and loam mixture to form strata-like layers. This nucleus should be faced with weathered stone, quarried stone, or rocks from old stone walls in such a way that many little niches, clefts, crevices, and terraces are formed on the sides of each hillock. Even here, natural strata must be kept in mind. All rocks should be set in a common main direction and all tilt at the same angle.

Since some alpine plants from higher elevations grow naturally in very meager soil, it is advantageous to work a heather soil into the upper part of the knoll. This soil is a dry humus and can be made of decomposed pine needles mixed with a gritty sand. Otherwise a good stone or gravel mulch is sufficient.

Karl H. Grieshaber has designed many well-known public and private gardens, including gardens at the New York Botanical Garden and Longwood Gardens.

Secrets of the Scree

by Eva Gallagher

Once you get involved in the nitty gritty of rock gardening, you will quickly come across plants associated with the intimidating phrase "require scree conditions." If you come from a background of perennials and vegetables, as most of us have, then the instructions for building this type of specialized environment are not just foreign, but seem to go against the grain of what constitutes good gardening.

Natural Screes

A scree is created by the continual freezing and thawing of water in rock fractures, which create smaller and smaller rocks from the cliffs and bedrock of the mountain—boulders into talus, talus into scree, (rock that is less than fist-sized and down to the size of crushed gravel), then to fine gravel and eventually to sand. If you have ever hiked across a scree slope, you will know how loose this substrate is, as your foot will slip and sink. In flat areas, it may be more settled, but it is still not enriched by any organic matter or clay, ingredients that are necessary to start the transformation of sand into soil.

The scree, then, is very free-draining, well-aerated (roots need oxygen, too!), and poor in nutrients. Water is never stagnant but always moving. The ever-present wind in the mountains also plays an important role, as it keeps the air in constant circulation around the alpine plants, whisking away any surface moisture. Alpines have adapted to these severe conditions by growing as mats or rosettes, often with fleshy or hairy leaves to preserve moisture, and often with tap roots that delve into the depths for water and for the few nutrients that may have been washed down from the surface. To grow these highly-adapted high-altitude alpines in your garden, you will have to duplicate their native conditions—by building a scree.

Although it sounds daunting, a scree may be one of the simplest projects to undertake in your garden and it need not take up a large area. We can all find a square meter or two and this will be sufficient for several dozen treasures. Be sure to have the scree next to a path or patio or it could even be the top surface of a raised bed-all locations where you will be able to see the plants close up. A slope coming from the base of a large boulder or outcropping makes a very natural looking scree. No slope? Many successful screes have been built on level ground by contouring it into gentle mounds and hollows.

Exposure

In the mountains the plants grow in full sun, but at our lower elevations we will have to provide some shelter from the heat of the noon-day sun, so a north east, north or north west slope is ideal. Alternatively, shade at noon can be provided by strategically-placed shrubs and boulders. Try to avoid placing the scree under trees not only because their roots soak up moisture and nutrients, but because they drop their leaves on the plants, trapping moisture and inviting decay. Remember, high alpines grow above the treeline and need just a blanket of snow to keep them dry in the winter. Choosing the windiest location in your garden will also help to mitigate the summer humidity.

You don't have the ideal site? Don't be put off. Mine is under trees, both pin cherry and jack pines. I get cherry suckers coming up, and flowers, unripe fruit, and leaves all fall on the bed along with the needles not only from the jack pines, but from nearby white and red pines. The plants still grow quite well, though maintenance is a nuisance as I have to remove all this debris—and needles are time-consuming to remove. A vacuum cleaner helps, though this tends to pick up the rock mulch which then has to be replaced. You also get funny looks from your neighbors when you spend Monday vacuuming your scree instead of your living room carpet.

Bottom Drainage

Most books recommend that your scree include a bottom drainage layer composed of at least 15 cm (6") of fist-sized rocks and coarse sand. This should be done if you have a clay subsoil, otherwise the roots of your plants will sit in stagnant water, especially if you have a level scree. I find that this is not necessary in my garden because I have coarse sand, and I don't have the continuous freezing and thawing that occurs during English winters.

"Soil" Mix

There are as many recipes for scree "soil" as there are experts—but one thing that they all agree on is the use of lots of gravel to provide that perfect drainage. The first step then is to visit your local quarry as you will need gravel in the 1/2-1 cm (1/4-1/2 inch) size. The scree bed should be 30-60 cm (1-2 feet) deep. Most alpines are not too fussy about pH, but a neutral or slightly alkaline scree will allow you to grow the widest possible range of plants, so mix and match your gravel accordingly. Granite results in an acid scree, and it has the disadvantage that it dries out faster than limestone or sandstone.

Reginald Farrer was a staunch advocate of the scree, "It is not too much to say that the discovery of the moraine and its possibilities has worked a second revolution in modern gardening." (You will find that the scree is often called a moraine or a dry moraine in early English rock gardening books. Today the term moraine means a scree with an underground water flow duplicating the snowmelt conditions at the edge of glaciers.) His recipe for a scree mix was one part alpine loam (made from two parts loam, one part sand, one part leaf mould and one part limestone rubble and crushed gravel) and five parts coarse gravel.

In his book *Rock Gardening*, H. Lincoln Foster recommends one part loam, two parts humus (peat, leaf mould and/or compost with a lacing of sheep manure and bone meal) and twelve parts coarse gravel.

The Siskiyou Nursery catalogue has this recipe for a lean scree: equal parts of coarse sand, gravel (both of which are free of silt) and leaf mould/peat.

Robert Bartolomei, curator of the rock garden at New York Botanical Garden, recommends a "mineral mix" made from equal parts of river bed gravel, coarse sand (such as is used for septic tank beds) and Turface (the red calcined clay that is used on sport fields). The Turface plays an important role as it is porous and absorbs not only water, but nutrients. He has used this with great success in his beds at NYBG.

The easiest scree of all to build is composed of 100% pure limestone gravel—again ½-1 cm (1/4-1/2 inch) in size. Fill the bed to a depth of one to two feet and that's it—you can start planting and looking forward to success after success. Skeptics take heed of the famous experiment done by noted British alpine gardener Will Ingwersen and described in his book

The Dianthus. He filled a large planter with washed limestone chippings, (sieved through a 1/4" sieve) and planted it with several different alpine species of *Dianthus*. Most "formed tight, hard and very characteristic cushions and flowered more freely than ever before." It takes courage to entrust your gems to pure stones and so some recommend first putting in a 10 cm (4") bottom layer of "goodies"—humus, rotting sods, or other nutrient-rich material.

My first scree was a total failure. My mix approximated the one recommended by H. Lincoln Foster, but with some sand added as well. The problem was that I used pure granite gravel, and the sand was acidic as well (there is just no limestone within 100 km of Deep River). I am not sure whether minerals just do not dissolve quickly enough from granite, or whether, together with the acidic sand, it created an environment that was too acid, but my alpines just didn't thrive. I waited unsuccessfully several years for the scree to work its miracle, but finally had to give up and rebuild it adding limestone and more humus. What a difference that has made!

Finishing the Scree
The final layer of your scree should be a 2-5 cm (1-2 inch) mulch of pure gravel—preferably of the same type as any boulders that you may have used. This helps to unify the area, prevent soil from splashing on the foliage (which could give pathogens a foothold), and allow air circulation under the mats, helping to dry out the plants and keep their crowns dry. More alpines are killed by hot humid weather than by cold.

I believe that a stone mulch is also critical to developing perfect buns—those tightly-packed rounded hummocks of foliage that alpine gardeners rave about. It wasn't until I had completely eliminated soil from the surface of my scree, did some of my plants start forming these attractive buns. Previously they would spread out into thin mats. Perhaps alpine stems instinctively need to come in contact with soil and so tend to grow laterally while soil is present. With gravel there is no possibility of rooting down, so the plants "pile up."

Maintenance
It is a good idea to top-dress each spring with a little peat, humus, gravel, and a lacing of bone meal. You will have to water in time of drought. A little water does a lot more good in a scree than in the garden loam, as the water can go directly to the roots. A scree, however, does not dry out as rapidly as you might think. Although the gravel on the surface heats up rapidly in sunlight, it cools down just as rapidly at night, allowing humidity to condense on the rocks and percolate back down.

That's it! Just remember—start off small. But I can assure you that, encouraged by your success, it will not be long before you take the advice of Roy Elliott, another noted English alpine authority, and start building "as many screes as one's energy or one's pocket permits."

Eva Gallagher is an Ontario area writer and gardener with a special interest in saxifrages and the rich Japanese flora

Rock Gardening on Level Land:
One Solution: the Plant Box

by Marnie Flook

Our present garden, in Chestertown, Maryland, was started when we moved in 1980 from a country property in Delaware to a city townhouse. Some plants from the original garden went to the townhouse, but others from that garden were transplanted here. When we changed our residence to Maryland in 1990 and left the townhouse, we moved as many plants as we could from the city garden to the present garden, which has continued to expand through the years. Now besides the areas planted with mature plants from previous gardens, there are woodland areas filled with wildflowers, rhododendrons, and other ericaceous shrubs; sunny borders planted with grasses, bulbs, perennials, shrubs and small trees; a low slope near the water where hundreds of daffodils bloom each spring; and several plunge beds for plants in transit.

The rock garden
It is difficult—almost impossible, in fact—to grow most of the real alpine plants in this location where the summers are hot, humid, and sometimes very dry, but many other rock garden plants do well. The land is flat and there are no rocks. Building a classic rock garden did not seem to be appropriate, but growing the plants in large boxes, basically raised beds, has proved to be entirely satisfactory.

The main "rock garden" area in our present property consists of two sets of plant boxes, similar but larger than ones we had in our former townhouse garden, situated by the side and the front of our house. The set in front of the house is the subject of this article. Because they are close to the house, and are also visible from our second-floor bedroom window, their plants are enjoyed as much as any in the garden.

On the first of November I looked out on this garden and was struck by the many shades of green in the two boxes—a lovely tapestry, maybe not as colorful as the spring picture, but very pleasing nevertheless. Before describing the plants, I want to say more about the boxes and how they came to be.

The original plant boxes
The inspiration for the plant boxes, which were the main feature in the townhouse garden came from the stone troughs we had photographed in Scotland in the Royal Botanic Garden, Edinburgh. This extraordinary place, especially the rock garden and alpine area, is probably familiar to many NARGS members. In this section there are groups of three or four beautifully-planted stone troughs of varying heights, arranged on a large terrace, each group surrounded by an appropriate ground cover.

We liked the different heights of the troughs and the way they were grouped together and decided to try something similar in our townhouse garden. Stone was impractical, so instead we built four planter boxes of different heights and sizes, using 4" x 4" pressure-treated lumber. One box was close to the house where it received some shade; the other three, interconnected in a pleasing manner, were built in the center of the garden, with a background of shrubs and trees. The sides of the boxes were lined with heavy black plastic to prevent the soil from drying out. The bottom part of the boxes was filled with rough drainage material and the top 12" with a mix of 1/3 good loam, 1/3 coarse builder's sand, and 1/3 peat moss.

A few rocks were carefully placed in the boxes and on each side to give the impression of a rock ledge. The dwarf conifers and small trees were placed first, then the rest of the rock garden plants were planted. A pebble mulch was added to give a neater finish and to keep the soil cool and moist. A few larger plants were placed around the boxes. This arrangement worked out well; each year some plants grew too large and some died, but most survived. The surrounding plantings softened the outside, as did the plants which trailed over the top.

The present plant boxes

We decided to build two similar sets of boxes next to our house in Maryland. In this article one of the two sets will be described in detail; the other set, by the end of the house, is very similar.

Both sets of boxes are made of 4" square, pressure-treated lumber, and the sides are lined with black plastic. The same soil mixture was used; a small amount of turkey grit was mixed in the soil as each plant was planted. A few small rocks were placed in each box for added interest. Both sets consist of one higher box interconnected with a lower one. Shrubs are planted on three sides. The fourth side of each group faces the path which goes between the boxes and the house. This arrangement of boxes containing over a hundred little plants is what I call my rock garden.

The photograph shows how one of the sets of boxes was constructed and how it looked before planting. The taller part is 5' wide, 8' long, and 18" high, and the lower part is 4' wide, 12' long, and 12" high. The boxes were stained with an opaque exterior stain before planting. Partial shade is provided by a nearby large red oak (*Quercus rubra*), a dogwood (*Cornus florida*), and a small Japanese snowball (*Styrax japonicus*). Several different microclimates are provided: the front of the larger box and most of the lower one receive sun part of the day; one end of the upper box shades the plants in the box below. Shade is also provided by two dwarf trees planted in the upper box.

Surrounding plants

The plants surrounding the boxes were chosen for their attractive, mostly evergreen foliage. A few perennials and bulbs were also planted. In front of the shady end near the house: *Rhododendron* 'Hardy Gardenia,' which has large white double flowers and handsome foliage; *Jeffersonia dubia* and *Jeffersonia diphylla*, whose ephemeral blue and white blooms don't get missed, since they are close to the house; *Eranthis hyemalis*, also placed where its early yellow flowers can be appreciated; later *Narcissus* 'Hawera,' a favorite dainty late-blooming daffodil cultivar from New Zealand, appears nearby, followed by several plants of *Astilbe chinensis* 'Finale' with feathery pink plumes.

In front of the two boxes, where it is sunnier, are several evergreen shrubs: *Calluna vulgaris* 'Sister Anne,' a low-growing heather with attractive, fuzzy foliage; *Rhododendron* 'Kazan,' a late-blooming Satsuki azalea formerly known as 'Rukizon'; *Buxus microphylla* 'Kingsville'; *Pieris yakushimanum*; and *Kalmia latifolia* 'Tiddly Winks.'

Also planted here is *Deutzia gracilis* 'Nikko,' a low-growing deciduous shrub which is beginning to spread too vigorously and may have to be moved. The yellow flowers of the fall-blooming bulb *Sternbergia lutea* give added interest at that season.

Pieris floribunda, the native pieris, is planted in the corner nearest the house where the two boxes intersect, along with another *Astilbe chinensis* 'Finale' and several plants of the dwarf *Hosta venusta*. At the far end of the lower box are a dwarf hemlock cultivar, *Tsuga canadensis* 'Stockman's Dwarf,' and *Pieris japonica* 'Bisbee Dwarf.'

Shrubs and trees in the higher box
First to be planted in the box were two Japanese maples, a red-leafed cultivar of *Acer palmatum* and *Acer palmatum* 'Viridis Dissectum,' a green threadleaf maple. These trees have thrived and are pruned each spring to keep them in scale with the rest of the planting. It may be a little extra work but they are so beautiful it is worth it. Another little tree in the box is *Ulmus parvifolia* 'Frosty,' a dwarf Chinese elm with tiny serrated leaves, edged with white. This tree also tends to get out of hand unless it is kept pruned.

The three dwarf conifers planted eight years ago have grown slowly and have kept their character: *Chamaecyparis obtusa* 'Nana,' *Chamaecyparis obtusa* 'Nana Lutea,' the yellow-leafed form of the dwarf Hinoki Cypress, and *Juniperus chinensis* 'Echinoformis,' the hedgehog juniper.

Shrubs in the lower box
No deciduous trees were planted in this box; the two dwarf conifers are thriving yet still in scale: *Tsuga canadensis* 'Jervis' and *Chamaecyparis pisifera* 'Tsukumo.' Several small ericaceous shrubs are shaded by the Japanese maple above: *Rhododendron* 'Ginny Gee' is a particularly floriferous plant: its buds are attractive from the time they form in early fall to when they open into beautiful, little pink flowers in the spring. The other two dwarf rhododendrons, *R. hanceanum* 'Nanum' and *R. keiskei* 'Yaku Fairy,' are growing slowly, but so far have had little bloom. Also thriving so far are *Polygala chamaebuxus*, a small shrub with pea-like yellow-and-white flowers, and *Chamaedaphne calyculata* 'Nana,' a dwarf leatherleaf with small pieris-like flowers in spring. Tucked in the corner below the upper box is the tiny *Pieris japonica* 'Little Heath Variegated,' a new addition this spring. All of these plants have evergreen foliage which looks good year-round. The only one I've had trouble with is the leatherleaf, which fared poorly several winters.

Rock garden plants in the higher box
Arabis x *sturii*	*Heuchera parishii*
Armeria caespitosa	*Hutchinsia alpina*
Aquilegia 'Fame Rose'	*Iberis candolleana* (now *I. pruitii*)
Campanula elatines ssp. *fenestrellata*	*Iberis pygmaea*
Dianthus 'Tiny Rubies'	*Phlox subulata* 'Blue Hills'
Erigeron scopulinus	*Pulsatilla vulgaris*
Helianthemum 'Amy Baring'	*Saxifraga veitchiana*
Heuchera hallii	*Veronica* 'Waterperry'
Heuchera 'Mayfair'	

There isn't space to discuss each plant but I want to comment on a few. *Arabis* x *sturii* has been a good choice; its clumps of bright green leaves have spread slowly in two corners, and its 4" white flower are an additional benefit in the spring. *Hutchinsia alpina* has always been a favorite with its ferny, dark green foliage and flowers like a miniature candytuft. *Helianthemum* 'Amy Baring' has produced its bright yellow flowers each year but has also had a few bad years when most of the foliage died. I like the way it cascades over the front of the box. The dwarf heucheras which are planted under *Acer* 'Viridis Dissectum' have been very successful; several clumps of *Heuchera* 'Mayfair' are now planted in the lower box in the shade of the same maple.

A warning about *Veronica* 'Waterperry,' which is planted in both boxes. It has year-round interest with its evergreen foliage which become slightly purplish in winter, and its spikes of blue flowers in the spring. In the boxes it spreads much too vigorously, however, and it needs to be restrained several times a year. I haven't decided to remove it yet, because many times I've needed a filler plant and have just pulled up a piece and replanted it. It always seems to live, and sometimes becomes a pest in its new location. It has another advantage of trailing its long stems over the box, softening the edges. It is a plant visitors always ask about when they see it in bloom in the spring.

Rock garden plants in the lower box

Aethionema grandiflora	*Geranium* 'Ballerina'
Aquilegia saximontana	*Heuchera pubescens*
Aquilegia species	*Iberis candolleana* (now *I. pruitii*)
Arabis androsacea	*Iberis pygmaea*
Arabis x *sturii*	*Iberis sayana*
Armeria caespitosa	*Lithodora diffusa* 'Heavenly Blue'
Aurinia saxatilis 'Tom Thumb'	*Orostachys aggregatus*
Campanula elatines ssp. *fenestrellata*	*Penstemon hirsutus* 'Pygmaea'
Campanula garganica 'W.H. Pope'	*Penstemon pinifolius*
Cyclamen cilicium	*Phlox* 'Coral Eye'
Degenia velebitica	*Rosularia pallida*
Dianthus 'Blue Hill'	*Thalictrum kiusianum*
Dianthus 'La Bourbille'	*Veronica* 'Waterperry'

The *Arabis*, *Heuchera*, and *Veronica* have already been described. Another reliable and fine little evergreen plant is *Iberis sayana*, certainly the nicest of the three small candytufts in the boxes. I find its mat of tight green foliage as attractive as its flowers. It is interesting that this is a plant propagated by Marcel LePiniec. *Iberis pygmaea* trails nicely over several corners in both boxes; *Iberis candolleana* is so small it probably should be in a trough. *Aurinia saxatilis* 'Tom Thumb' was planted in the lower box eight years ago. Through the years its branches have become thick and gnarled, just as promised in the Siskiyou Rare Plant Nursery catalog. It now covers a 12" square space on the edge of the box with more of its branches trailing below. The yellow flowers appear in spring, but it is the plant's appearance the rest of the year that appeals to me.

One of the most delicate-appearing but actually quite rugged plants is *Thalictrum kiusianum*, which always seems to come up later than expected every year. After six years its underground runners have spread in and among the small ericaceous shrubs,

Phyllis Gustafson's Czech crevice garden in Oregon. *Photo by Phyllis Gustafson.*

Gwen Kelaidis dryland garden in Colorado. *Photo by Gwen & Panayoti Kelaidis.*

Gwen Kelaidis dryland garden in Colorado. *Photo by Gwen & Panayoti Kelaidis.*

Troughs at Royal Horticultural Society, Wisley. *Photo by Dick Bartlett.*

Conifers integrated into the rock garden. *Photo by Jim Cross.*

Marnie Flook's plant boxes before planting. *Photo by Marnie Flook*

Plant boxes in bloom. *Photo by Marnie Flook*

Sand bed in the Slater Pennsylvania garden. *Photo by Michael Slater.*

creating a dainty ground cover of tiny leaves and little pink fluffs of flowers. Just beyond, still in partial shade, is my plant of *Lithodora diffusa* 'Heavenly Blue,' one of the more temperamental plants in the garden. I am very fond of its beautiful, deep blue flowers and its narrow dark green foliage; I've almost lost it several times during particularly cold winters. One wonderful spring it bloomed in profusion, but usually only a few flowers appear at the end of the trailing stems at any one time. It blooms from spring until fall, and even now in November, one stem still has three brilliant blue blossoms.

Orostachys aggregatus and *Rosularia pallida*, two fascinating succulent plants, are spreading in the crevice between two of the small rocks that were added to this box. *Campanula elatines* ssp. *fenestrellata* has formed a solid green mound of attractive, serrated leaves. Not at all restrained was another campanula (probably a form of *Campanula poscharskyana*) which somehow got into the far end of the box. This spring I finally pulled out every piece, which involved redoing that part of the little garden. The replanted *Iberis, Penstemon,* and *Geranium* all survived but so did a few more little plants of the errant campanula—or rather they had survived until I saw them this morning.

The other plant boxes
It would be easy to keep writing about the individual plants in these boxes. The two sets contain a similar mix of little shrubs and plants. Another *Acer* 'Viridis Dissectum' is planted in the upper box, shading several rhododendrons and a dwarf hemlock. Two more small hemlocks are planted in the box below along with *Rhododendron* 'Patty Bee' and *Pieris japonica* 'Bonsai.' In a bit more sun are *Pinus mugo* 'Valley Cushion' and *Ilex* 'Piccolo.' These boxes are surrounded by a larger area planted with many ericaceous shrubs.

Disadvantages
Soil tends to compact and settle in these small areas and has to be replenished; plants have to be kept under more control than in a large garden and may need to be watered more often.

The advantages of plant boxes
Accessibility: it's easier to get to plants; being by the house means the plant are enjoyed all the time; control of soil mix is facilitated, and many plants can be grown in a small space. In short, these boxes have proven to be an attractive and practical solution to rock gardening in a level place with poor soil and a difficult climate.

Marnie Flook is the long-time archivist for NARGS and gardens in Chestertown, Maryland.

Walls: An Interview with Ellie Spingarn

by Gwen Kelaidis

How did you get started building walls?

When I first married, I found myself living in a house perched on an outcrop of rock. I had grown up in Danbury, Connecticut where the soil was rich and deep, but nevertheless I liked the rock. In fact, I love the look of stone. Next thing I knew, I was building a ledge into a rock garden. One thing led to another and I began building with stone. Projects became larger – quite large, in fact. The rocks were there, a beautiful granite rock of varying shades from steely blue to almost yellow.

The Brooklyn Botanic Gardens guide on garden construction was my best book. There was also an article on wall construction by Frank Cabot in the ARGS Bulletin about the time I started.

If you build walls right, the work will still be there when you depart this earth. In the meantime, you have the pleasure of living with the finished product. There is little maintenance, since seeds can only reach the soil between the rocks when carried by wind or the sticky body of a slug. You can stand nose to nose with alpines growing happily. The only problem, really, is that you eventually run out of wall that hasn't been planted. Then you need to build more.

What was your first big project?

I had built a few garden walls before, but my first big project was the stonework on the house. When we moved in, the house was little more than a shed-like cottage, perched on blocks at the corners. I built a retaining wall 5' high and 40' long on one side. Then we jacked up the house and took out 1,000 yards of fill, and I built the foundation underneath.

The first big garden project was the retaining wall for the kitchen garden. I wanted to create a level area where there was originally a slope outside the back door.

What was your method?

In our area a 3' footing is recommended to give stability in the frosty soils of winter. I dug a trench 3' deep and 3' back into the slope. I put in a layer of stones, fitting them together, then cemented the joints, and fit the stones for the next layer. You can do this layer without concrete, and -by fitting the stones closely – get just as much stability. Now I don't use cement in the joints anymore, but rather sand and pea gravel. This actually provides better drainage. Stability is a must, however. You should be able to walk on the rocks in the trench without any of the rocks shifting from your weight. I have met stone masons who just dump rocks in the trench, but I don't believe that walls built on such a foundation would stand the test of time. Use any "clunkers" here in the trench -any rocks that are unattractive or don't have a good face. Work up to 4-6" below the ground and then start building.

You need batter boards to guide the building of the wall -straight boards to place at each end of the wall. Drive nails in each board every 6" – the two boards should have identical spacing of nails. Set the bottom of the boards exactly at the front of the wall.

Pitch the boards back to the desired top front of the wall. I use a batter of about 1" back for 1' up. Tie strings between the first two levels of nails to show you where the face of the rocks should be. As you place each rock, the face of the rock comes up to the string and not beyond. Try to get the whole of the flat face of the rock in the plane of the string, so that the face of the wall is absolutely straight. Never violate the plane of the front. Use two strings at a time so that you can draw a bead between them. As the wall grows, move the strings up.

It is critical that every stone in the wall be stable. Use chinks wherever necessary for stability. Very often you can find scraps or cut a rock down. Backfill the wall as you go. My backfill has gravel added to it for very good drainage. The backfill mix should extend about a foot behind the wall. The back of the wall will be irregular. With heavier soil, you may need a drain pipe here and there at the base of the wall.

How do you choose which rock to place next?
Building a wall is a lot like fitting a puzzle together. Aim to find a stone with a fairly good face, if not a great one. Consider the stones around the one you are placing. Mix sizes as well as shapes and don't put too many small ones in any one area. I work each layer for the entire length of the wall before building up. As you add another layer, stagger the rocks in layers so that there is never a crevice over a crevice.

I strive to lay each stone level. The middle line of each stone is level. Even if the stone is oval, keep a horizontal line in mind. With irregular stones, eye through the middle of the rock.

How can you build such high walls? Do you work from the top?
Even at the top of a 7' wall retaining a slope above, I do not work from the top of the wall. It isn't possible for me to get a good fit that way. I use scaffolding—cinder blocks with boards across them.

How do you get your stones to fit so well? How do you get such a flat face?
I chisel just about every stone. Mostly I chisel the edges to make them fit well, but I also take knobs off the faces. I use a 3-lb sledge with a short handle, called a cold chisel. Chiseling is good and it's bad. The uniform faces and close fit that result make a very handsome wall, but the crevices are then very narrow. It's almost impossible to replace plants when they die. You can choose to deliberately leave pockets in the wall for planting.

Anyone is going to learn an awful lot the first time he/she builds a wall. You're going to ruin some good stones—sometimes more breaks off than you think. My rock is a granite, or I've been told, a schist granite. I don't know anything about it, but the rocks do differ in color and density. Some you can't chisel.

Do you take any precautions when you are handling the stone?
I don't wear safety glasses, although I do wear glasses, but you should be cautious. Do as I say and not as I do. Be careful when you are trying to break a rock. On my clumsy days, I've picked up a blister or two. Work on a firm surface, always. The rock must be very stable when you are hitting it.

You have to learn how to pick up rocks. Don't take any chances. Don't stand up with straight legs and try to pick up a heavy stone. Bend your legs into a squat, grasp the rock, and then stand up, bringing the weight up with the strength of your legs. Be very careful. You've only got one back. If you hurt your back, all the fun of building walls is over.

I wear gloves, always, when building walls. I like rubber gloves because they grasp the stone best and they're thin. I got started using these because of the cement work. They are a must when working with cement. I use a wheelbarrow mixing either soil or cement.

My rocks weigh up to 100 pounds. I have used much larger rocks near the bottom of the wall. There I can use crowbars and rollers to tumble them into place. If you look closely at my walls you will see that there are more large rocks near the bottom.

How long does it take you to build a long wall?
Some days I get more done than others. It seems like I find wonderful fits at first. Then suddenly nothing fits; I can't find the right rock. I have learned to work on something else when that happens. I get a lot more done that way.

One long wall was started on Labor Day weekend and I worked on it every day as much as I could. I got it about 4' tall by spring and gradually finished it by the following year. There are 55 cubic yards of stone in that wall.

It took two years to do the foundation of the house. Those stone walls were about all I did those years—aside from caring for two small children!

When do you plant the wall?
Of course, as you are building the wall you are planting it. After each layer of rock in the wall, fill the nooks and crannies and sprinkle a layer of soil over all. I screen the soil before using it, usually with a 1/4"-3/8" screen. This means the minimum depth of the soil layer is 1/4."

Plant and water plants as you go. I use a mist from a garden hose to water the plants if they have to be watered again.

Rooted cuttings or same-year seedlings are most desirable. A young plant can find its way, sending roots into the crevices. It's better not to bare-root plants if you don't have to. The plants start growing immediately. Replacements in a closely fitted wall must be tiny seedlings.

What soil mix do you use in the crevices?
You only have one chance to mix the soil in the wall. You can't replace it later without tearing the wall apart.

It's not good to use much sand because when the soil dries out, the sand will dribble out. I use loam of a light texture, peat moss, compost, and bone meal (because my soil is acid). I test it as I mix it. I want soil that will barely hold together as a ball when squeezed hard. Plants seem to grow very well in this mix.

What time of year do you plant?
Spring is the ideal time to plant a wall. The plants are eager to grow then. Early fall is also good, into October in warmer parts of the country. If the construction of the wall is loose and there are wider crevices between rocks, the wall could be planted after it is finished.

What are some good plants for walls?
Good plants for walls include *Campanula portenschlagiana, C. garganica, C. cochlearifolia,* and *C. poscharskyana.* All are good, although the latter can be invasive. Alpine primroses—the auricula group, pubescens hybrids, *P. marginata*— are all good.

I'll try pieces of things not considered wall plants. *Gentiana scabra* and *Daphne arbuscula* have both done well for me.

Anything that grows in crevices in nature is an ideal candidate for wall culture. Plus be adventuresome—try other things. I even have a cow parsnip, 8' tall, that seeded into a crevice. It normally grows in damp places and ditches.

What sort of maintenance problems have you had?
I haven't had trouble with rodents in my walls. Once a rat lived in one because it was a convenient and short commute to the nearby bird feeder, where grain was so easily obtained. From time to time, ants will inhabit the walls. I suppose one could poison them, but I have never bothered. I have so much wall.

Walls never need to be painted and many of mine have needed no maintenance whatsoever. I do have one wall where the soil has washed out. This one would benefit from a gutter in the gravel terrace above it. When we have heavy rains the water runs right down the face of the wall. The roof gutters of the house empty out directly onto the gravel terrace, so this is an extreme situation.

Why don't more people build walls?
Not everyone has access to stone and purchasing it is prohibitive. And it is hard work to build walls. I used 80 cubic yards of backfill for the kitchen garden wall.

Yet done one day at a time, the wall is finished in surprisingly little time, as long as you work at it every day. It's very satisfying, very rewarding. I thank the moon, the stars and the whatever that I have the materials, the interest, and the go-power. Do just a little bit at a time, never more than you feel comfortable with.

Ellie Spingarn is a long-time member of the NARGS and the Connecticut chapter. She gardens and builds walls near West Redding, Connecticut. She was interviewed by Gwen Kelaidis in January 1991.

Gardening in Sand Beds

by Michael Slater

I grew up watching westerns on television and reading Zane Grey novels. Both of these sources made "The Wild West" alluring to youngsters like me. This adventurous and romantic notion of what the west is still influences me strongly. These days, however, instead of yearning to run off to Wyoming and become a cowboy, I yearn to grow the plants that fit into my mental image of the West.

Deserts, dry plains, canyons, mesas, buttes, colorful rocks, and defiant vegetation: this is what I want to have a little bit of here in my garden. My goal is to grow plants that remind me of the dry parts of Colorado, Wyoming, Utah, or Idaho right here in the Mid-Atlantic States. Many plants from sections of Asia, Southern Africa, and South America with cold winters and hot dry summers are also highly desirable. Thousands of species and varieties of great rock garden plants come from these climates. In the wild these plants, from *Acantholimon araxanum* to *Zauschneria latifolia* v. *garrettii*, routinely survive temperatures well above and below what we have in our garden so they should be growable, but………

Summer wetness and humidity encourage fungal growth and rotting of many plants. For weeks on end, in July and August, we often have temperatures of 90°F to 100°F (32° to 38°C) with humidity greater than 80% in the middle of the afternoon. When such high humidity is present the night-time temperatures often stay above 80°F (27°C). Winter can be a problem if water from frequent winter rains or melting snow stands around the plants. A beautiful little plant can rot and turn to mush after only a day or two of such weather.

Dry sand beds are one answer. Dry sand will help plants from low rainfall climates resist moisture and humidity problems partly because there is NO organic matter at the surface or in the top several inches which can harbor fungi. Plants from dry climates have not co-evolved with the vast array of fungus found in our damp part of the world. The sand should also drain away all water and dry rapidly at the surface. And deeper down, the porosity of the sand will bring adequate air, and thus oxygen, to the roots of the plants. I certainly can't claim that dry sand is the only way to go, but it is certainly one good way.

In the history of the *Rock Garden Quarterly* and its predecessor the *ARGS Bulletin*, there have been only two articles about dry sand beds. It has been 50 years since Carlton R. Worth first wrote about western plants that throve in dry sand even though he neglected them during WWII. And it has been 18 years since Norman C. Deno described how to make and utilize a dry sand bed. Professor Deno followed this with a significant chapter in *Rocky Mountain Alpines*, the magnificent and indispensable book compiled for the 1986 Interim International Rock Garden Meeting in Boulder, Colorado.

This is where I first learned about dry-sand beds for growing western plants. The list of plants grown was tantalizing and included eriogonums, western phloxes, penstemons, drabas and acantholimons. I soon had the exciting opportunity to visit Norm's garden the following spring. I will never forget how he demonstrated the toughness of his six-foot diameter mat of *Eriogonum umbellatum*, by just laying down on it! After that I had to make a sand bed for myself! I say make rather than build because little building is usually needed.

Dry sandbeds are such an easy and successful system for growing drought-loving plants that I am puzzled as to why more people don't have one as part of their rock garden. Maybe it is because we rock gardeners have a great fascination (obsession?) with soil mixtures, formulas, and recipes. We just KNOW that if we could just find the right formula or the correct secret ingredient, we could grow anything! Sand beds don't satisfy this need at all, since sand is the only ingredient. How disappointing! Nothing to mix, no careful layers to lay, nothing but sand.

Here are the complete instructions for turning a flat, level, sunny lawn into a dry sand bed:

1) Kill the grass (and weeds). Use glyphosate and wait a week or use any method you find acceptable.

2) Put down an even layer of sand 6-8 inches deep (15-20 cm). I have used as little as 4 inches in part of one bed and 12-18 inches in another case and both seem to grow plants well.

3) Optional step: Add rocks in whatever quantity and arrangement pleases you and fits your budget.

4) If your new sand bed is in contact with remaining lawn, a barrier is desirable to keep grass rhizomes from invading. See any basic gardening book for ideas.

5) Optional step: Create an edge out of some hard material like stone or land-scape timbers, to keep the sand neatly in place, thus creating a low raised bed. Avoid making your sand bed raised too high, it will be TOO well drained and nothing but true desert plants, like cacti, will grow there.

6) Plant your plants.

If you are interested enough to have read this far, you probably have some questions:

What kind of sand should I use?
I prefer what is called builders sand in our area. It is the sand generally used to make concrete. It contains a mixture of particle sizes from medium sand up to little pebbles. My first sand bed was made with a fine-grained, even-sized particle sand called masonry sand (the kind used to make mortar). Norm Deno also has a sand bed made of masonry sand. The plants grow contentedly in it, and the only problem with it is rain splashes, which coat the smaller plants with sand. I added a thin stone mulch to alleviate this problem.

How much sand should I buy and how will I get it home?

The supplier you buy from will be able to tell you how much the sand you are buying will weigh per cubic yard. You must then apply a little simple geometry to calculate how much you will need for the square footage and depth of the bed you are planning. Be prepared for a big truck! Our latest sand bed measures 8' x 40' and is about 12" deep (OK, maybe 18" deep in spots) and needed about 16 tons of sand. I had ordered 18 tons but they had as much on the truck as they could get. If you buy enough sand, the delivery is free. Have the delivery truck dump it where you want your bed if at all possible!

Don't the plants need some food?

First, even small plants will quickly send their roots down deep, and they can grow into the original soil which hasn't been disturbed.

Second, I scatter a little bit of time release fertilizer tablets around every other year (or three) just to give the plants a little bit more food. But mainly I like the plants to stay small and tight. Lush plants would be out of character in this type of garden.

(John Good, from Wales states that he uses a formula created by E.B. Anderson many years ago. It consists of 6 parts bone meal to 1 part sulfate of potash. He scatters the mixture over his scree beds in late winter, where rainfall washes it in. It is very easy on the plants and won't burn the foliage.)

How much sun is needed?

Two out of the three sand beds I have get NO SHADE at all from 8 am until 5 pm, and we are on a slight, south-facing hillside, so the sunlight is about as intense as possible here in Pennsylvania. The third bed gets shade from about mid-afternoon on. (I have seen one sand bed on a north-facing slope, in another garden, that didn't dry out at the surface for many days after any rain. The owner has a great deal of trouble with liverworts growing on it.)

My garden is on a hill. What can I do? Doesn't the rain wash the sand away?

Several of my sand beds are on a slope (5 to 10 degrees) and I have used rocks with as little space as possible between them to make terraces down the slope. Under the influence of rain and time the sand tends to be "self-leveling" and must be held back like water behind a dam. I have found many plants that do well plugging these vertical crevices so sand can't wash through. Sempervivums, rosularias, and jovibarbas are particularly good for this position.

Use sand with little pebbles in it (like the builders sand mentioned above), and you will find that rain will wash away the tiny grains from the surface of the sand leaving behind the largest grains and tiny pebbles making a nice (but thin) gravel mulch with no work on your part.

Sand color changes over time. The sand I receive is usually is a funny, yellowish color when it is delivered. The surface soon gets bleached by the sun to a light grey which is very effective at showing off the plants.

Can I dig out a hole and fill it with sand to make a dry sand bed?

I found I wanted to do exactly this when I made sand beds at the top of an existing mortared stone wall along our driveway. For me it works just fine. I simply dug out about 12" (30 cm) of soil, threw in a little bit of organic matter in the form of compost 0.5 to 1" thick (1-2.5 cm) since there was only poor subsoil left at the bottom of the hole. The rest of the void was filled with sand. This can only work if the surrounding soil is a very well-drained, like the sandy loam we have. I have no real problems to report, but the lowest end of one bed does stay damp for a couple of days after a rain and only in that spot do we have any trouble with weed seeds germinating. On moderately- to poorly-drained soil, I think you must either raise the bed above ground level or install an underground drainage system.

What is the best time of year to make and plant a dry sand bed?

The bed can be made in any season. I have found planting in the summer is very difficult in a dry sand bed. Keeping plants watered well enough to get them established is even more difficult than it is in a regular garden. Planting in the spring and Fall is much more successful. So if you build one during the summer, while you wait for the fall planting season to arrive, be prepared to have your neighbor asking you why you have built a giant sandbox in your yard. Of course once you start tucking in hundreds of little plants, they will think you are even crazier than they had previously suspected!

Will I ever need to water?

Probably not. I don't water at all, except for one or two plants close to the house that probably don't really belong in a sand bed.

What kind of rock can be used in a sand bed and how should they be placed?

The rules and recommendations on rock garden design in *Rock Gardening* by H. Lincoln Foster are a good place to start. For my sand beds, I used our local, reddish sandstone-conglomerate. I like the rock's color, it strikes me as very "Wild West," and I have been able to get it when I need it. Just remember the sand's surface is "self-leveling" and no slope can be maintained over time without placing rocks for terraces or putting on a thick gravel mulch.

I have found that my dry sand beds give me great pleasure and make an easy and relatively carefree way to grow dryland plants here in Southeastern Pennsylvania. There have been only a few problems which I will mention.

Neighborhood cats may come to view your sand bed as their own giant litter box. Their "activity" can easily smother small treasured plants. When this happened, I found that covering the favored area with chicken wire easily discouraged the feline activity. Over the first 7 or 8 years of my sand bed gardening, this was a very minor problem. Then a new and very determined cat moved in next door. When I covered his selected spot with chicken wire, he just moved to the next available space. Commercial cat repellent failed, as its label predicted, to change the cat's established behavior. In the end I resorted to covering the entire bed with a shield of chicken wire and turkey wire. I found the turkey wire, with its 2" (5 cm) holes to be harder for cats to walk on. This actually didn't look too awful, but I felt deprived of contact with my plants. I couldn't reach them to pick off a dead leaf here or pull a little weed seedling there. Early the following spring I began preventative measures. I took a large number of dried hot peppers (*Capsicum* varieties) and ground them finely in an electric coffee grinder I use for spices. I mixed this hot, red pepper powder with diatomaceous earth. Then I used our vegetable garden duster to spread the powder over the entire sand bed. With re-application after any rains the cats caused no problems at all last year. Caution: Stay upwind and don't breathe this very irritating dust!

Weeds growing from seed are no problem at all. If any do germinate and grow, they are incredibly easy to pull out. The sand is delivered free of weed seeds, so weeding is much less of a burden than in any other garden I have. As I mentioned above, weed seeds that blow into the beds only seem to germinate in the one spot where the surface of the sand stays damp for several days after a rainfall. Rhizomatous grasses are another story. They can be an incredible nuisance if they get into your sand bed. But of course that is true of any "normal" rock garden. An ounce of prevention is worth a pound of cure, so I recommend either an industrial strength weed barrier or careful edging with glyphosate herbicide.

People who live in dry climates with low humidity may get a chuckle out of reading all of the preceding. What I go through to grow dryland plants here in the humid eastern part of North America is, I suppose, like people in Denver who try to grow rhododendrons and primulas. It isn't completely futile, but is it worth the trouble? Yes, the dry sand bed is more than worth it! (However, I can't really tell you about rhododendrons in Denver.) Not every dryland plant will be happy in my climate, but with guidance from past pioneers I have found dry sand beds to be a relatively carefree way to grow many of the dryland plants I desire.

The variety of plants which have done well in our dry sand beds is very large. The vast number of choices really give me a chance to travel by the seeds I plant. A brief survey of a few of the outstanding performers follows.

Buns look great in a sand bed and many which are considered difficult grow will grow very well there. Choice species of *Acantholimon, Dianthus, Draba, Gypsophila,* and *Arenaria*, perform a fine imitation of sea urchins in a tide pool. *Acantholimon* has been one of the outstanding genera in my sand beds. They get very little in the way of brown spots in the cushion, and they have beautiful, but spiny, leaves. *Acantholimon araxanum* and *A. ulicinum* (syn. *A. androsaceum*) are my current favorites. *Draba cappadocica* is the best of the crucifer tribe I've grown from seed lately. The golden flowers barely rise above the somewhat fuzzy grey bun. Several little *Gypsophila* have good foliage and make good buns in the sand bed, but don't bother growing them for the flowers. *Gypsophila tenuifolia* has nice, sort of grass-like leave and sparse pinkish flowers on stems around six inches tall. *Gypsophila aretioides* needs far too many adjectives for the size of the plant! It is the most amazing 4"-wide, rock-hard, little grey mound. People who haven't seen it before can't help touching it, but neither can the owner. Ours had 2 (yes, TWO) flowers several years ago. The best thing that can be said about them is that they didn't obscure the wonderful bun!

Mat-formers like *Veronica oltensis* and *Thymus neiceffii* add a different note that I like. Be wary of fast spreaders like *Veronica liwanensis*. It looks fine, but it wants to take up far more space than I am willing to let it have.

Little daisies are wonderful and there are a few of the most choice ones which really seem to thrive in dry sand. *Townsendia jonesii* is a superb mound with large and very pale lavender daisies nested in the foliage. It also appears to be truly perennial in addition to setting a large amount of seed. It is the best *Townsendia* I have grown. The yellow flowered *Erigeron linearis*, at about 4 inches (10 cm) high, is very nice (watch out for the forms without ray flowers!) The very tiny *E. scopulinus* is the most wonderful little *Asteraceae* of all. Grow it in any sand bed, rock garden, or trough!

Grey-leaved plants give a special flavor to any garden, but their contribution to the character of a dry sand bed is exceptional. Try *Helichrysum splendidum*, *Hymenoxys subintegra*, or *Artemisia frigida* if you really want to knock the socks off your visitors.

Eriogonum is one of my favorite genera. Some of the tiniest and most appealing ones are growing wonderfully in dry sand. *Eriogonum kennedyi* varieties *alpigenum* and *austromontanum* are the smallest, greyest, and tightest little mats I grow, after *Gypsophila aretioides*. *Eriogonum umbellatum* v. *porteri* is a great small form of this ubiquitous western sulfur flower. I could go on and on but I will content myself with mentioning *Eriogonum strictum* v. *proliferum* with fascinating grey or grey-green spade-shaped leaves which instead of holding them out flat like most plants, it twists the stem 90 degrees so the leaf blade is perpendicular to the ground. It makes for an interesting effect. I assume this is an adaptation for coping with too much solar radiation in its native habitat.

Bulbs and other plants which go dormant in the summer seem to do very well in dry sand. *Lewisia nevadensis* and *L. pygmaea* are mainstays in my latest sand bed. Many varieties of *Crocus* and bulbous *Iris* thrive. I have put some *Calochortus* seedlings in, and they are still present after two years. I wonder how long they will take to bloom?

Shrubs, sub-shrubs, and dwarf conifers in small numbers accent the nearby tiny mats and buns. This helps the sand beds seem a little more wild and less artificial and garden like. *Cowania mexicana* (a stiff upright shrub from the Southwest), several varieties of *Calluna vulgaris*, *Arctostaphylos uva-ursi* (both East Coast forms and a form from Alaska), plus a few small and interesting dwarf conifers like *Juniperus chinensis* 'Shimpaku' are all welcomed in and are thriving. Remember the native soil is not that far down, and these shrubs will have their roots down there quickly, so you can consider any shrub which you know grows well in your area in full sun.

Succulents, of course, are in their element! *Cactus, Delosperma, Sempervivum, Rosularia, Orostachys,* and *Sedum* are incredible and indispensable. Try *Echinocereus baileyi, E. viridiflorus, E. caespitosus,* and *Coryphantha vivipara* if you like wonderful little ball cactuses. *Delosperma nubigenum* and *D. cooperi* are reliable through every winter for us, and I keep trying all I can from seed. The succulent foliage is nice, and the incredibly bright colors of the flowers are great. *Delosperma congestum* seems like it is going to be the next good doer. As mentioned above, *Sempervivum* and its cousins make good plants to hold back the sand in vertical crevices. I prefer selections with grey or reddish foliage, which complement my red rocks and grey sand.

Penstemon large and small are spectacular against my large reddish boulders. Although not considered among the most difficult and desirable of the *Penstemon* clan, *Penstemon cardinals, P. strictus, P. barbatus,* and *P. palmeri* make tall colorful spikes. Lower down, *Penstemon linarioides* v. *coloradoensis* put on a good display of clear, light blue flowers above narrow grey leaves, while *Penstemon pinifolius* make dense forests of its small pine-like foliage well decorated with bright red flowers. The lowest of all is *Penstemon caespitosus* 'Claude Barr' with small blue flowers nestled in its ground-hugging mat of leaves.

Quite a few plants with interesting foliage can be grown in dry sand, and they will lend an exotic air to the bed. Try *Cheilanthes fendleri* in the north side of a rock where its roots can stay a little bit cooler. The small grey daggers of the leaves of *Yucca harrimanae* make it look good in small groups. In the dry sand mine all have leaves less than 6 inches (15 cm) long.

Lastly, both alphabetically and in grandeur of floral display, the queen of the summer in our sand beds is *Zauschneria latifolia* v. *garrettii.* The mound of grey-green foliage covered with red-orange trumpets in August and September makes it worthwhile to sacrifice the space for this 3-4 foot wide (1-1.3 m.) plant. *Zauschneria* has been sunk into *Epilobium* by taxonomists recently. This name change will have to stick and be accepted before this gardener changes his labels! I like the name *Zauschneria,* and it doesn't look like an *Epilobium* to me!

Some of the plants which have done well for me in dry sand beds with full sun (no shade at all) and no supplemental water even during our drought last summer:

(Disclaimer: I don't claim this is the only place to grow them successfully)

Acantholimon araxanum, A. acerosum, A. armenum, A. bracteatum v. capitatum, A. dianthifolium, A. glumaceum, A. hohenackeri, A. ulicinum (syn *A. androsaceum*), *A. venustum* (several young plants seem very happy)
Achillea ex 'King Edward'
Aethionema oppositifolium (syn *Eunomia oppositifolia.*)
Alyssum caespitosum
Alyssum propinquum
Arabis androsacea, A. bryoides

Arctostaphylos uva-ursi

Arenaria hookeri, A. saxosa (name not verified (n.v.) looks a lot like *A. montanum*), *A. pseudoacantholimon* (n.v.), *A. stellariana, A. tetraquetra, A. t.* var. *granatensis* (scorches some during the summer, but survives)

Armeria juniperifolia (syn. *A. caespitosa*), *A. girardii* (syn. *A. setacea*)

Artemisia frigida

Asperula gussonii (*AGS Encyclopedia* says it should have bluish foliage ...ine is bright green. Do I have *A. nitida*? I do water this one occasionally, but I'm not sure if it really needs it.)

Bruckenthalia spiculifolia

Calluna vulgaris 'Dainty Bess,' *C.v.* 'Minima,' *C.v.* 'Mrs. Ronald Grey'

Cheilanthes fendleri

Conradina verticillata

Cowania mexicana

Delosperma aberdeenense, D. cooperi, D. macei (n.v.) and *D. nubigenum* (sm. yellow flowers)

Dianthus freynii, D. petraeus ssp. *noeanus* (syn *D. noeanus*), *D. simulans*

Draba cappadocica, D. densifolia, D. rigida imbricata (how do I tell this from *D. bryoides*?), *D. rosularis*

Echinocereus triglochidiatus, E. viridiflorus

Ephedra frustillata, E. minima, E. minuta, E. sinica

Erigeron aureus, E. compositus, E. elegantulus, E. scopulinus, E. simplex

Eriogonum caespitosum, E. douglasii, E. ericifolium v. *pulchrum, E. jamesii, E. jamesii* v. *flavescens, E. kennedyi* v. *austromontanum, E. kennedyi* v. *alpigenum,* (*E. ovalifolium* v. *nivale* and *E. o. v. purpureum* seem to live through two years, bloom and die. More seedling are coming on though!), *E. strictum* v. *proliferum, E. umbellatum, E. umbellatum* v. *porteri*

Erysimum kotschyanum

Genista 'Vancouver Gold,' *G. sylvestris* (syn *G. dalmatica*)

Globularia cordifolia

Gypsophila aretioides, G. tenuifolia

Helichrysum splendidum

Hudsonia ericoides (none lived more than 3 years, I will keep trying.)

Ipheion uniflorum

Ipomopsis aggregata (This seems to be monocarpic for me, so I keep starting seed from the seed exchanges.)

Leptospermum humifusum (a hardy Tasmanian!)

Lesquerella alpinum, L. arizonica, L. kingii

Lewisia nevadensis , L. pygmaea, L. rediviva

Origanum libanoticum

Paronychia sessiliflora

Penstemon angustifolius, P. aridus, P. barbatus, P. barbatus (yellow form), *P. caespitosus, P. cardinalis, P. caryi, P. davidsonii, P. eriantherus, P. fruticosus, P.* hyb. (purple, from *P. barbatus* + ?), *P. laricifolius* v. *exilifolius, P. laricifolius* v.

laricifolius, P. linarioides v. *coloradoensis, P. jamesii, P. kunthii, P. neomexicana, P. palmeri, P. pinifolius, P. procerus* v. *tolmiei, P. secundiflorus, P. strictus, P. virens*

Petrophytum caespitosum, P. hendersonii

Phlox 'Pink star,' *P.* 'Schneewitchen,' *P.* 'Tamanonagelei,' *P. diffusa, P. hoodii, P. pulvinata, P.* 'Tiny Bugles'

Physaria alpestris

Pinus sylvestris 'Hillside creeper'

Pterocephalus pinardii

Ptilotrichum spinosum (syn *Alyssum spinosum*)

Rosularia 4 or 5 species

Sempervivum many varieties (good for between rocks to hold back the sand in the terraces of sloped sand beds)

Teucrium marum

Thymus neiceffii

Townsendia exscapa, T. incana, T. jonesii, T. parryi, T. rothrockii

Veronica bombycina v. *frederyana* (variety n.v.), *V. liwanensis, V. oltensis*

Viola pedata, concolor and bicolor forms

Vitaliana primuliflora (recovering nicely from the vole attack)

Yucca glauca, Y. harrimanae,

Zauschneria latifolia v. *garrettii* (Syn. *Epilobium canum* v. *latifolia*)

Michael Slater lives and gardens in Mohnton, Pennsylvania. He has a deep interest in woodland wildflowers, as well as the plants of western North America.

Gardening in Shade: A Technique Worth Trying

by Jim McClements

Growing plants successfully in shaded areas, either woodland or shady rock gardens, is often not as easy as it would seem. Even if the right plants are chosen, shady areas are often not as fertile as they appear, either because the soil beneath the surface is poor and/or poorly drained, or because of significant root competition, particularly of shallow-rooted trees such as beech, maple, and tulip poplar. While digging a small hole and dropping in a woodland plant will work in some situations, one often finds that more is needed.

We have had a gradually enlarging woodland garden for about fifteen years, initially containing mostly wildflowers of the eastern U.S., but now including many western and Asiatic species. It, therefore, came as a bit of a shock when several years ago I found out that I had been doing it all wrong!

This revelation was the result of reading a summary of an article by John Neumer, of Hockessin, Delaware, the original of which was published in *The Dodecatheon*, newsletter of the Delaware Valley Chapter in 1986. I think it will be of interest to any gardener, but particularly to those who struggle in a woodland setting to provide an ideal situation for plants, namely, one free of tree-root competition while combining maximum organic material with good drainage. While my experience with John's scheme is relatively short, I am much impressed and will describe results thus far, a few ideas on modifications, and a recent update from its originator.

First, let me insert here the original article by John:

The Peat Bed
by John Neumer

Primulas are worth a little extra effort: a peat bed perhaps? The British and Louise Beebe Wilder discuss their peat gardens as if every garden setting has one, of course. One imagines great borders filled two feet with peat and sand—borders which certainly I will never have. And then, too, as before every new effort, there is always some doubt. A British gardener surrounded by chalk requires a verisimilitude of woodland earth; but did Louise have a similar compelling need? Well, put such doubts to rest. Even a compromise "peat" bed requiring only modest effort has powers to please that will astonish even the inveterate gardener. So momentarily stop your labors of re-creating a mountainside (it will never work anyway) and enjoy the relative play of establishing a 50 sq. ft. "peat" bed. You will quickly repeat the effort, but try this modest bed first.

In late fall, preparation begins by selecting a turfed area under high, one-half day shade. Don't touch the turf. Pile oak and other available leaves to a depth of 1.5-2 ft. over the new border profile, and relax until spring. Then, with the leaf mass now compressed (an occasional winter stamping helps), I distribute over the leaves coarse sand and 160 lb. of composted cow manure. Think of building a layer cake. Sixteen cubic feet of peat and a thin overlay of coarse sand complete the effort. Other than spreading the individual layers more or less evenly, there is no mixing of the layers.

The capping of the bed is done sufficiently early for the spring rains to wet the bed thoroughly. If I'm ambitious, I add a top cosmetic layer of woodland scruff, but this is not necessary. The bed is now ready for spring planting. When planting primulas, I use a collar of loam to anchor them in the loose bed. This is important, you will see, for winter security. In one season the bed medium takes on a black color like that seen in wet Rocky Mountain vales. I never thought that I could find thrills in root structure, but when you lift a *Primula* cluster and see the vigor of the white threads deeply penetrating this black mass, you know you have created a very special environment. Maintenance is easy; every year I add a thin layer of leaves, peat, and coarse sand.

The bed is also a "natural" for a host of Japanese woodlanders, and for virtually every other subject which dawdles elsewhere in the rock garden. In my experience, more "new" gardening goes on in these beds than in the rock garden proper. This year the peat bed was the first to receive *Boenninghausenia albiflora* and *Roscoea alpina* seedlings, and here they have prospered. It is an ideal refuge for Japanese polemoniums, aconitums, and select gentians. The propensity of this bed for accommodation is, I'm sure, endless: all young azalea cuttings are given a year of two in the bed before their final setting. And not least to mention, it is the only proper home for the phlox woodlanders.

I am ever thankful that a few of the fine Ohio basin woodland phlox subspecies collected by Rocknoll Nursery persisted in my garden long enough to find their "proper" home in the "peat" bed. For the first time I now see them as their genes intended, and what a spectacle it is! For this show alone, the bed would be worth thrice the effort.

Discovering the peat bed is a little like an artist finally becoming aware of the medium in which he can express exponential creativity. You come to realize that almost no area of the rock garden is ideally suited to its plant inhabitants (the rock wall is the one exception that proves the rule); most of our subjects merely tolerate their transposed environment and we in turn are rewarded with struggle and angst. Peat bed gardening by contrast is natural gardening at its best; it cooperates with all natural tendencies within the suited subjects. This symbiosis is never better than in the peat bed. For East Coast gardeners, the rock garden rewards, but the peat bed rewards overwhelmingly.

A final caveat: the above construction of the peat bed is an evolved design. At first I dug out a bed and filled the hollow with peat, sand and manure. This bed gave inordinate heaving of Primulas during winter. Thus the leaf mold base offers an important root anchor. Nevertheless, even in the new beds, I also use a loam collar around new sets as additional anchoring insurance.

Here are my modifications and comments:

I started the first of these beds by piling up leaves in December 1995. The bed was completed in April, in time to receive most of the spring arrivals from various sources. By the middle of summer, I was so impressed with the way everything was thriving that I went ahead with another bed, using left-over mulched leaves from the previous year as the base. Two more beds followed shortly thereafter, and more the following year, so that I now have eleven and am working on more!

Almost everything has done well, from ferns to *Arisaema* to *Phlox* to *Primula* to *Trillium*. For instance, in May of 1996, I transplanted new seedlings of *Glaucidium palmatum*, an act reputed to be a real "no-no" (but better than watching them damp off!). I was gratified to see them all survive. A dwarf *Kalmia* bought at a meeting and found to have essentially no roots when unpotted, flowered the following year. Ferns grown from spore and set out are soon mature plants, and I can confirm John's observations about the huge root systems that develop readily in these beds. They are equally as valuable as nursery beds for seedlings and newly acquired plants as they are for mature plantings, and they should be used both ways.

As for modifications, I have tried two. The first is to use a layer of the woven "weed fabric" under each of the beds (under the leaf pile). This is for further insurance against the intrusion of tree roots, particularly those of tulip poplars, which have in the past few years been the bane of our existence. After years of laboriously double-digging woodland beds and chiseling out roots, it dawned on me that what I was mainly doing was stimulating more root growth! It is important not to dig or disturb the ground where the peat bed is to be located. The bed can be put at the base of a tree, but should not cover more than a quarter or so of the tree's root area.

My second idea was to use some Turface (calcined clay) in the upper layer of sand. I discussed this with John and he agreed that it might help, particularly if one can't obtain coarse builders sand. (Fine sand is not what you want.) I've stopped using the Turface, however, mainly because it made the consistency of the top layer too loose, which not only allows for more frost heaving, but worse, encourages squirrel digging. I've recently started topping the beds with a composted pine bark material obtained from Lowe's (a general building supply store). This acts as a moisture-retaining mulch, adds organic material, and is neat and attractive.

I tried to pin John down on the thickness of the various layers, but he apparently varies that to some extent depending on what he has "lying around." The bottom sand layer should be about 2 inches, the peat layer 4-6 inches and the upper sand an inch or so. (I find that John's recommended 16 cu. ft. of peat for a 50 sq. ft bed is a bit much). He says that the real secret is NOT to skimp on the leaves, which will shrink considerably over a few years. His recommended yearly addition of leaves, peat, and coarse sand goes on in the late fall after plants go dormant.

I asked if he had rodent problems. The answer was "no," but I have recently found some vole activity behind the logs that I have been using to edge the beds. (Without edging they look somewhat as if an elephant has been recently buried.) I think that the voles will be easily controlled with poison, but I may be overly optimistic.

My final question to John, who has been using this approach for over ten years, was about long-term results and problems. He is still as enthusiastic as when he wrote the article, and just completed a very large peat bed. He does say that some of the beds tend to "peter out" in about five years, particularly if the initial leaf layer has not been generous enough and/or if the yearly replenishment has not added enough organic material. In that case, he transfers the plants to another bed while redoing the first one.

I've constructed most of my beds over a short period of time, rather than over a winter. This is done by using already composted, chopped leaves and by taking the time to thoroughly wet the peat moss <u>as the bed is being put together.</u> Beds thus constructed can be planted immediately.

Is it possible to substitute something else for peat? There is serious question as to whether advocating ANY use of peat in the garden is appropriate in the face of the rapid depletion of this resource, particularly in North America. Products made of coconut shells have been suggested by some as a peat substitute, but reports of contamination with pathogenic organisms have made me hesitant to try. I'm currently experimenting with substituting the composted pine bark mentioned above for the peat layer in the "sandwich." It's too soon to know, but I'm hopeful that results will be equally good.

These beds are easy to construct (especially compared to "double-digging!"), give wonderful results, and should be of special appeal to those who are forced to garden in clay soils, as are found in Delaware. They have certainly changed my approach to gardening.

I currently grow species of the following genera with great success in these beds: *Trillium, Arisaema, Hepatica, Cypripedium, Shortia, Glaucidium, Paris, Podophyllum, Asarum, Epimedium, Helleborus, Jeffersonia, Primula, Polygonatum, Disporum, Thalictrum, Anemone, Anemonella, Phlox, Tanakea, Tricyrtis,* and *Uvularia,* dwarf species of *Kalmia, Pieris,* and *Rhododendron,* and many woodland ferns.

Jim McClements gardens with his wife Anne in Dover, Delaware. He is currently Recording Secretary of NARGS, and has served as Chair of the Delaware Valley Chapter. He was a co-founder of the internet list, Trillium-L, in 1997.

The First One Hundred: Recommended Plants for Beginners

by Geoffrey Charlesworth

When you finally arrive at rock gardening, there seems to be an overwhelming number of plants from which to choose. Do more expensive plants give more pleasure? Is it better to go for the inexpensive ones and get more plants for the same money? Shall I start with a color scheme in mind? Shall I collect a single genus? Shall I grow exactly what X or Y is growing? (The answer to all these questions is No). I started out by wanting a beautiful rocky outcrop with colorful mats flowing over the rocks and delightful buns tucked into pockets of soil between the rocks, with a few taller plants for variety. My ideal would start flowering in early April and continue nonstop through September at least. Maybe this is your aim too. How to do it?

Without some experience, growing plants from seed is a lottery and hardly a viable way of filling a garden as quickly as an eager beginner would like. Then there are plant sales at the chapter meetings. You can get excellent bargains and excellent plants too, but it is not a swift and reliable way to fill a garden. You can't expect to find at a sale the particular plant you have just seen or read about and have set your mind on growing. There is no point in taking your want list to a sale. The chance is too remote that anyone else knows what you want or could supply it if they did. The best way to get something you want is from a reliable mail-order nursery, but you still may have to adjust your want list to what is available. Of course you must visit local nurseries too, to find out what is available there. The plants you buy there will probably establish better than plants that have been subjected to the indignities of air travel. But once you open a mail-order catalog you realize that the world of plants is far bigger than your local nursery can handle.

Here follows a list of plants that are "easy." That is, they will probably prosper if you give them reasonable care; they are also easy in the sense that they are obtainable. It is not a comprehensive plant list for beginners, I am recommending plants that I would recommend to a friend who was just starting out and wanted advice to follow or ignore. The virtue of these plants is that they were available recently and will probably be available for several years, as they all have durable value. I ransacked all the catalogs that arrived in January and February to look for the plants that everybody should grow. Sometimes I give the description offered by the nursery and sometimes my own experience. There are many other plants other than rock garden plants offered, but I have included only plants suitable for a rock garden which has relatively good drainage, plenty of sun, and is free from the competition of shrub and tree roots and large perennials with big leaves. Some plants are woodlanders and will be described as shade plants. You can decide whether to have a special woodland area or whether to try them in the shadier spots in your rock garden. In any case, the soil for them would need to contain more humus and not drain as rapidly as for alpines.

Most of the plants we grow from seed are species; they are plants you would expect to find in the wild. If an observant gardener finds a plant with some unusual quality, such as larger-than-normal flowers, double flowers, or variegated leaves, he or she wants to spread it around. Plants grown from seed nearly always vary from each other and from their parents, so the only reliable way to propagate a special plant is vegetatively—by cuttings or division. Such a set of plants is called a clone. The best distributors of such clones are nurseries. They have the skills and equipment needed to produce the hundreds of plants of each good form or hybrid which will satisfy the nation's gardeners. Most forms and hybrids are given fancy names designating them as having a special quality that most wild plants don't have. Not only beginners but more experienced gardeners are always on the lookout for new and good forms. I like to try out every new plant I can find and afford, to evaluate it against my own idea of beauty and interest and to see whether it likes the conditions in my garden.

I shall not recommend many clones explicitly because to appreciate an unusual form you ought first to know what the standard wild form looks like. But don't be deterred from getting a named form—that may be all that is available. Besides visitors who know only the standard species will be fascinated to see an unusual color form or a dwarf form growing in your garden. There is one caveat: if every plant in your garden is a large-flowered form, a double-flowered form, or has variegated leaves, the garden will not look very alpine. It will lose its innocence and appear artificial. This may be the effect you want, and that is fine. But if what you really want is a natural mountain-top effect, sooner or later you will have to grow the species plants, and that probably means growing some plants from seed. Nurseries also propagate many alpines from seed, and the absence of a fancy name implies that even though the plant may have been propagated from cuttings it is a true species and not a man-made hybrid.

In the following descriptions of the plants I have quoted excerpts from some of the fine descriptions of the nurseries themselves. A quote from a particular nursery doesn't mean that the plant is only available there. Some nurseries don't write descriptions at all. A list of mail-order nurseries follows, and you might want to do some comparison shopping, although there is no way of comparing quality and size without seeing the plants. There are also many good nurseries that I have never used. More importantly there are hundreds of plants a beginner could grow, and this list is meant to lead you on rather than limit your vision.

The authors of these affectionate puffs are unknown and will be designated by a letter showing the name of the nursery. But I imagine Baldassare, Betty Ann, Nancy, Evie, Dick, Rene, Eleanor, Marty, and all the other nursery operators will give credit to their writers. It is fascinating how different eyes notice different aspects of the same plant.

S = Siskiyou Rare Plant Nursery; R =Rice Creek*; M = Montrose*; NG =Nature's Garden; C.= Cricklewood; W = WeDu; RK = Rocknoll; WR = Woodland Rockery; CA = Colorado Alpines* [*no longer selling by mail. Ed.]. Any remark not in quotes is my own opinion.

There are several other good nurseries selling these plants. The ones listed above have the best descriptions.

Achillea ageratifolia. "A permanent mat of little silvery lance-shaped leaves and numerous white-petalled flowers with off-white centers. The white-on-white effect is most appealing." S. "A cheerful plant." WR. There are a number of useful yarrows. This one is as large a plant as you would want in a small rock garden, and you could even use it at the front of a border. This has better flowers than most. This *Achillea* is often called *Anthemis aizoon*.

Actinea herbacea: "Large yellow daisies on a dwarf plant makes a bright accent in the spring garden" R. This plant is described as a form of *Hymenoxys acaulis* (see later), which is essentially a high mountain cushion but is also a plains plant about six inches high and takes up as much space as *Aster alpinus*. Could even be used as a front of the border plant.

Aethionema 'Warley Rose'. "Dwarf shrub for hot, dry positions. Tiny colorful blue-green leaves smothered in rose-pink. *Daphne*-like blossoms in May and June." S. "Evergreen bushlets with *Daphne*-pink rosebuds." RK. This plant is probably a form of *A. armena*. Other aethionemas such as *A. pulchellum* are just as good, but you may have to start them from seed. They may then self-sow attractively in cracks and crannies. 'Warley Rose' is a good color but never produces seedlings for me.

Aethionema grandiflorum: "The steel-blue, needle-like foliage is lovely all winter, and in spring heads of delicate pale pink flowers are produced. Give it sun." M.

Aethionema oppositifolia: "One of the tiniest woody shrubs known. A delightful plant that creates a flat even mat of grey, fleshy, round leaves less than an inch high. Short stems carry heads of pale lavender flowers in very early spring. A hardy plant from the mountains of Lebanon." S. It has lived for me through the harshest of winters without protection. The leaf-flower color combination is ravishing, and it blooms with the earliest drabas. It may be listed as *Eunomia oppositifolia*.

Ajuga: Don't plant ajugas in your rock garden. The only exception might be a form of *Ajuga* usually called 'Metallica Crispa`. "Curly bronze leaves. Non-spreading. Looks like red dwarf spinach." R. "Speckled silver and purple curled and shiny leaves." RK. "A foxy specimen plant for a partially shady area. It's composed of congested crinkled leaves with a purplish sheen that emit short racemes of deep-blue flowers." WR. There is also a form with redder leaves.

Alchemilla alpina: "Dark green foliage with silver edge and reverse." C. This is primarily a foliage plant. The flowers are greeny yellow. At its most attractive after rain when drops of water sit in the upturned umbrellas. The leaves are quite large for a small rock garden. *A. mollis* is more often seen, but it is far too large and weedy for a rock garden. Both species merit space only if you are very fond of leafy landscapes.

Anacyclus depressus: "Wheel-like patterns of lacy, greyish-green foliage develop white, red backed, daisy-like blooms at their tips." RK. There is a good reason to get this from a nursery; the seed you get from exchanges is very rarely viable. This beautiful daisy comes from North Africa and southern Spain, so you wouldn't expect it to be hardy in Massachusetts. It survives and self sows.

Androsace lanuginosa. "A vigorous, easy plant from the Himalayas with silvery trailing stems ending in clusters of lavender pink, white-eyed flowers. Valued for long summer bloom. Zone 4." S. "Easy Himalayan." CA. This is one of the few *Androsace* that are perfectly happy outside. It is not a bun and not really a mat, but it needs a foot of room to sprawl around. The stems don't seem to root down.

Androsace sarmentosa: "Hardy Himalayan species with hairy, silver foliage rosettes that spread by stolons densely covered with light pink. *Verbena*-like blossoms in April and May. Zone 3." S. This is the first *Androsace* to plant and a never-ending source of delight. You can move bits of it around when it roots down. There are a number of forms equally good. *A. primuloides* is the same or a very similar plant. "Makes a patch of furry buttons that sends up quantities of pink flowers in May. Even out of bloom the silvery rosettes are attractive." R. *A. sempervivoides* is neater but not so reliable.

Anemone x *lesseri*: "Bright red flowers. Will grow to 12" in maturity. Likes a moist soil in sun or part shade." R. It doesn't actually need moisture. The color is unusual since most rock garden anemones are white.

Anemone multifida: "Full sun, good drainage. Elegant finely-divided foliage; cream, red or yellow colored flowers on long stalks in late spring. Native to the Rockies." W.

Anemone nemorosa: "An endearing early spring blooming wildflower which carpets woods and shady hillsides of N. Europe to N.W. Asia. The species has lovely white flowers, light pink reverse. Plant the woody rhizomes horizontally, 2in. deep." S. There are several color forms from white to deep blue and red, also some doubles. A broad sheet of them in a woodland would be great, but the pretty forms look good singly in a shady part of the rock garden.

Anemonella thalictroides: "This native perennial is happy in a woodland setting or in a shaded rock garden. The blue-green foliage provides a collar for the delicate white to pink flowers. It grows from a tuberous root and occasionally reblooms in the fall; however it disappears during the summer. To 9" but usually much shorter. Zones 3-10." M. "Extremely delicate in appearance, but tough and long-lived in the garden. White or pinkish anemone-like flowers in earliest spring; often bloom sporadically through the season." W.

Antennaria dioica: "Dwarf carpeting, mountain plants, easy in full sun and well-drained soil." S. "Flat silvery-white mats." RK. Pussy-toes is a spreader but easy to control. The flowers of some of the forms are worth having; the usual species flower is a little dingy. It adds a grey patch to the green mats of summer.

Aquilegia bertolonii: "One of the smallest and finest. Large rich blue upturned flowers." S. There are a number of miniature aquilegias for a beginner. Taller ones also are at home in the rock garden, but there is a good deal of crossing goes on and the subsequent self-sowing will give you a mixed bag of sometimes uncontrollable seedlings. Some people want this effect, but once you have it, it is hard to change.

Aquilegia flabellata: is probably more permanent than *A. bertolonii*. "A wonderful Japanese native well suited to our climate. It grows to about 15" and blooms with blue and white flowers in early spring. The lovely, blue-green foliage is more resistant than most to leaf miner. Semi-shade. Zones 3-10." M. "Fleshy fringed foliage produces 3-4" stems of long-lasting deep blue and white flowers with recurved spurs. Blooms early summer. Prefers a cool position." CA. "Prefers a mostly sunny site." WR. Note the differences between advice from North Carolina, Vail CO, and Michigan. In Massachusetts it doesn't mind sun. There are dwarf forms, some all white.

Arabis ferdinandi-coburgii 'Variegata': "A valuable foliage *Arabis* forming a mound of neat rosettes of 1in. creamy-white leaves, each with a narrow center zone of green. White flowers on 5 in. stems." S. Another *Arabis* you can get from any local nursery is *A. caucasica*. This is not to be despised but must be kept tidy by shearing and not allowed to ramp unchecked. There is a variegated form of this too but *Arabis ferdinandi-coburgii* is neater, though the flowers are not as good. Another name for *A. caucasica* is *A. albida*, and there is a double form "which blooms all spring and makes an effect like popcorn. An old-fashioned plant that has become rare." R.

Arenaria montana: "Clouds of large pure white flowers smother the plant in early summer. Attractive dark green foliage year round. Alps. Zone 5, but grown in Zone 4 with winter mulch." S. "Myriads of white cup-shaped flowers. Foliage is deep green needle-like in mats. Classic rock plant." R. This is one of the best sandworts for flowers. I have found it impermanent without protection in the Berkshires, but I have seen it growing very happily in Hartford a little bit south of here. Arenarias on the whole are easy, but this one is worth a little extra trouble.

Armeria juniperifolia (= *A. caespitosa*): "Minute hummocks of leaves. Long lasting white flowers nestle right on the foliage. 2"." R. "Dense buns sprout short stems topped with papery, rose-pink flower-heads. This little fellow prefers a mostly sunny area with a well-drained soil." WR. "Spherical pink flowers rise just above the foliage." CA. White and pink forms are first-rate plants. Perhaps the best of the thrifts. When it begins to look shabby after a few years, you can easily propagate it by pressing tufts of foliage into sand.

Armeria maritima: This is a plant of wide distribution on both sides of the Atlantic. It has white, cherry-red, and pink forms. "Foliage makes a fine-textured grassy mat." R. "The fine, evergreen leaves will form a tight bun, and you will be rewarded with heads of mauve-pink flowers in spring." M.

Asarum hartwegii: "The cyclamen-leafed ginger is doubtless one of our best native plants. Green leaves with conspicuous silver veining. Requires extra gritty, woodland soil. Succeeds even in Zone 4 though usually rated zone 6." S. Indeed it is hardy for us. This is a woodlander with large glossy leaves, but it might be happy in a shady, moist spot at the foot of a cliff.

Asperula gussonii: "Compact cushion of short, needle-like leaves which become covered with small, fragrant pink flowers." CA "A mini-mat of dark green leaves nearly hidden by the abundance of small, tubular, flesh-pink blossoms in late spring." WR.

Asperula sintenisii (= *A. nitida* var. *puberula*): "Makes a light green cushion smothered in a sheet of pink tubular star flowers in spring. Zone 6." S. Actually both these asperulas seem to be OK in Zone 4-5 if they are planted in fast draining scree. Keep trying until you get one of them established. I have heard it said that hairy-leaved *A.*

suberosa would also survive with proper care but I have only been successful with this in the alpine house.

Aster alpinus: "Daisies in spring above clustered leaves." R. Color forms vary from deep mauve, pink, and white. At least one color should be found in everybody's garden. Note that most other asters bloom in the fall and this distinguishes them from *Erigeron*.

Astilbe chinensis 'Pumila': "A nearly flat mat of heavily dissected foliage and 10-12" spikes of fuzzy, shocking-pink blossoms. A dependable summer bloomer for a partially shady rock garden." WR. Or you can put it in a woodland setting where it is vigorous enough to fend for itself. Most of the *Astilbe* cultivars only look right in a border or formal woodland garden; this one has a natural look but gives lots of color at a low point in the year.

Aubrieta deltoidea: "Classic rock plants." S. The forms of this species are legion and splendid. Plant several to find out whether you like the reds or the lilacs or near blues. The one with variegated foliage was easier to establish for me than many of the hybrids from England. They are easy enough from seed, but you will get some of the less clear colors. If you succeed with growing this species from seed, go on to other species of *Aubrieta* which are less flashy but very good plants.

Aurinia saxatilis: Basket-of-Gold is obtainable at any local nursery. There are some color forms, pale yellow and even a buff color. Also double and compact forms. "Pale moonlight-gold flowers. Soft grey-green foliage." RK.

Bolax glebaria: "Glossy green leaf rosettes make an intriguing armor-like pad. Little yellow flowers." S. "Tough, plastic-like, glossy green foliage produces a low, spreading mat." CA. True for both the normal size plant and the tiny leaf variety. In shade the "pad" is more lax but is a refined ground cover like an out-of-flower mossy saxifrage.

Callirhoe involucrata: "Full sun; good drainage. Midwestern native. Procumbent plant with long trailing stems, forming a loose mat. Beautiful, silky wine-colored flowers over a long period in midsummer." W. Winecups is the common name. It sprawls around the rock garden without doing much harm to its neighbors.

Campanula barbata: "Flat foliage rosette, pale blue fussy bell flowers." C. This is a short-lived perennial and may be biennial in your garden, but it seeds around sensibly.

Campanula carpatica: A very dependable campanula, a little on the large side but well within acceptable size for a rock garden or a wall garden. It will self sow quite readily and forms extensive colonies but also will sow itself charmingly in crevices that are otherwise unplantable. "It blooms all summer just like an annual." R. "Compact tufts of heart-shaped leaves." RK. The white form is pretty, too.

Campanula cochlearifolia: "Fairy children of dusky blue on 2" stems. Spreads into a nice patch." R. "Profuse, dainty, bell-shaped light blue flowers. Needs well-drained soil." CA. In my experience it runs around at random invading but rarely harming other plants. It may die out so let it go where it thinks best. Some forms are difficult to establish.

Campanula kemulariae: "An easy, valuable groundcover and wall plant for shade, under shrubs, even in dryish soil. From a creeping rootstock rise tufts of shiny leaves and foot-long pendulous stems carrying many big open blue bells in June." S. "Showers of deep lavender bells just above attractive glossy leaves." R. "Toothed leaves and decumbent 10-12" stems of good- sized bluish-mauve bells. It is best grown in a sunny wall, or where it can cascade over rocks." WR. I have it growing and mingling with *Geranium dalmaticum* and both survive their close relationship. The blue is good and goes well with the pink of the *Geranium*, the color may depend on soil and exposure. In another raised bed it flows poetically over the sunny side but also tries to creep backwards into the drabas and other small fry. It has to be periodically restrained.

Chrysanthemum weyrichii : "Large pink daisies hug the shiny deep green carpeting foliage in late summer." R. "Year round a neat spreading plant of cut shining green leaves and in summer 3" wide pink daisies on 4" stems. Ideal running through crevices of a sunny wall." S. "Darling pink daisies." RK. "Leathery, glossy green foliage." CA. "a spattering of pink, daisy-like blossoms in late summer." WR. It always takes me by surprise in mid July. It hugs a large rock next to a path and runs along the base in a long line not trying to invade the path. The flowers are summery pink but the size of fall chrysanthemums, and it looks like a rock plant, not a bedding chrysanthemum.

Chrysogonum virginianum: "Yellow daisies above bright green foliage mats." R. "This is a splendid long-blooming native plant which is happy in sun or shade. It produces bright yellow flowers from early spring through fall and is nearly evergreen with leaves disappearing only after extreme cold." M. "Six inch quarter sized gold buttons. April to frost." RK. "Lavish clumps of hairy green leaves and bright-yellow flowers...well-drained soil that lcans towards the acid end of the scale. It should do fairly well in a mostly sunny garden if it is not allowed to go bone-dry during the summer." WR. A composite with lots of character and a useful carpet-former at the edge of a wood. The low form is superior and more commonly found.

Claytonia virginica: "A delicate native plant, less than a foot high which thrives in shade or sun. Growing from a corm, it makes a brief appearance from winter into very early spring. The flowers which are pink or white with pink stripes are produced in racemes." M.

Cotoneaster apiculata: A good small shrub for a small garden. Plant it next to a rock and watch it mould itself to cover the rock. 'Tom Thumb' is a good dwarf form; "An elfin form of the 'Cranberry Cotoneaster' with dainty near-oval leaves. Quite slow growing, but will root where its little branches touch the ground and form a small mat after a few years." WR.

Cyclamen hederifolium: "Makes colonies of marbled leaves." R. "This is one of the hardiest species. The beautiful leaves are infinitely variable even on a single plant and the white or pink flowers are produced occasionally during the summer and in abundance throughout the fall." M. You may have trouble with *Cyclamen* if animals discover the corms. The wrong combination of cold and wet may decimate them, but grown in the right place there is nothing to compare with a sweep of *C. hederifolium* or in a warmer spot, *C. coum*.

Cytisus decumbens: "Low shrub, 6-10" tall by 3-4' wide. Bright yellow flowers." CA. There are a number of good rock garden brooms. Some will provide medium-sized shrubs for large accent. Some are spiny. A good hybrid which some catalogs have sometimes is *C.* x *kewensis*. Grow something near brooms that self- sows a little, such as *Erinus alpinus* or *Chaenorrhinum oreganifolium*, so that when the shrub expands you won't need to rescue anything precious.

Daphne cneorum: A lovely sweet scented low shrub. After *D. mezereum* this is the most often seen in gardens and therefore has less rarity value than the cultish species that can be troublesome to grow and hard to find. But it is probably the best of them all. *Daphne mezereum* is one of the first plants to flower in the whole garden and therefore worth keeping in spite of its slightly weedy habit. *Daphne cneorum* never misbehaves except to die off in patches without adequate explanation. "Covered with masses of intensely fragrant pink flowers." CA.

Delosperma nubigenum: "Full sun; good drainage. Very low-spreading; succulent, yellowish foliage; bright yellow-orange flowers in June." W. "This succulent-leaved plant makes a fine ground cover in a sunny location. It is drought tolerant and non-invasive, producing bright yellow flowers in spring. The vivid green foliage turns red in the winter sun. It is 1" high and hardy enough to grow in the Denver Botanic Garden." M. Yes it is hardy for us, too. Other delospermas, South African natives, are not hardy here but are worth trying a little further south. Try for instance *D. cooperi*. "Hardy in Denver but not in Vail." CA.

Dianthus: Grow several of the alpine species, for instance *D. freynii* ("stiff, grey-green leaves" CA.) *D. gratianopolitanus* ("Tight cushions, fragrant" CA.), *D. microlepis* ("tight carpet, nearly stemless" R. "Green, curved, needle-like leaves" CA.) *D. nitidus* ("Bright green rosettes ... shiny pink flowers ... dark calyx" CA). *D. petraeus* ssp. *noeanus* ("spiny buns...reminiscent of shimmering fireworks" WR. "white fringed flowers" R.), *D. simulans* ("tufts like pincushions" R). *D. subacaulis* ("grey-green ... nice pink" CA) If you don't mind losing a plant soon after it blooms with only a sporting chance of having it a second year, grow *D. alpinus*. Also grow a few of the many dwarf hybrids such as 'Little Joe', 'Mars', 'Tiny Rubies' ("tiny double rosy carnations" R.), but not the larger hybrids, unless you can find a place in the border for them. Anything that looks like a carnation looks wrong near rock plants. *D. deltoides* has some good color forms but can become a nuisance when it produces endless seedlings of indifferent colors.

Dicentra cucullaria: "Dutchman's Breeches. Snowy flowers like little pantaloons hung out to dry in the April woods." R. "Racemes of nodding, 2-spurred white flowers." W. What you get are tiny rhizomes. Plant these, watch the leaves disappear and understand that you will have to wait until next April to see them. Meanwhile, they sit for most of the year just underground, so mark the spot and don't disturb or slice them inadvertently.

Dodecatheon meadia: "Delightful cyclamen-like white or pale pink flowers on a tall spike in May; basal rosette of narrow leaves." W. "Robust eastern species that retains the firm green leaves well into summer." S. You will need a location that retains some moisture for this. Everybody should grow some representative of the emblematic genus of NARGS, and this is one of the easier species in the East. *D. pulchellum* is OK, too.

Draba dedeana: "Pure white flowers on 2" stems. Small, wide bristle-tipped leaves. Spain and the Pyrenees. One of the best species. Zone 4." S. Most of the white drabas are rather dull plants, and the good drabas are nearly all yellow, so this has two advantages.

Draba lasiocarpa: "Forms a small hummock of most unique foliage. Stiff, green, pine needle leaves. Racemes of pale yellow. Eastern Europe mountains. Zone 5." Southern Zone 4 is OK too.

Draba oligosperma: "Small, rigid, grey-green leaves form tight rosettes which huddle together in a hard cushion." CA. *D. lasiocarpa* and *D. oligosperma* are just two of many species of draba blooming before the crocus and into May. Get several species to compare the tight foliage of the buns and mats. If you succumb to Drabamania you will graduate to growing them from seed. Some need protection from winter wet, but most are hardy through the worst weather.

Draba sibirica: "is one of the easiest species to grow in a mostly sunny site." WR. And therefore needs a special mention, because it makes quite extensive mats and not just tiny buns.

Dryas octopetala: "Easy and beautiful. Large white flowers and silky seed heads. Most attractive dark, mottled foliage makes a neat ground cover." S. "Evergreen creeper with large white flowers like single roses. Leaves like miniature oak leaves." R. Probably best in a sandy scree in our climate. Some gardeners grow enormous mats of *Dryas*, but mine gets damaged each winter and takes time to revive in spring.

Edraianthus graminifolius: "A stunning crevice plant featuring especially thin grassy green foliage. The violet-blue flowers are abundant on prostrate stems." S. There are many subspecies of *E. graminifolius* from different geographic locations with small differences. All the kinds I have grown have been excellent, and the abundant self-sowing they do is welcome. *E. pumilio* is even prettier but not so amenable. "Beautiful violet-purple trumpets in late spring." CA.

Erica carnea: There are so many varieties of heathers that some nurseries specialize in *Calluna* and *Erica*, and devotees form societies to exchange cultivars and cultural information. Plant a few specimen plants at first to test your site for soil (it should be peaty and never dry out totally) and climate (some member of the family will grow in most parts of the US and Canada). Collecting forms can be addictive.

Erigeron compositus: "Bright lavender flowers on dwarf downy foliaged plants an inch high." R. You can expect to get a plant of *E. compositus* at most plant sales. Since it is variable, a plant from a mail-order nursery is probably going to be a good form. In any case you should plant several forms of this western daisy.

Erigeron scopulinum: "Rock crevices. Small white daisies. Excellent for troughs". S. The small leaves make a tight mat, and the daisies are not very numerous but look just right.

Erinus alpinus: "Rose purple flowers." RK. Will self sow into cracks and crannies, but it is small enough to be harmless to most of its neighbors. There are white and pink forms.

Eriogonum umbellatum: "An attractive mat of green, silver-backed leaves and tall stems of cream flowers in July." S. "Can form mats or sub-shrubs." CA. It is very variable with forms of differing size, color and habit. But it is one of the easier buckwheats.

Erysimum kotschyanum: "This excellent plant soon forms carpets of yellow over tight foliage. An easy and valuable plant for any sunny position." S. Most erysimums are short lived, even biennial. This one is "permanent" and divides easily to spread around. I have never found seedlings though. Its disadvantage is that it resembles a draba, and one would like different genera to look different.

Genista delphinensis: "Short flattened stems make an interesting effect. Yellow broom flowers. Zone 4." S. This plant makes a mat that is impossible to weed. If weeds get out of hand you will have to dig up pieces and replant them. But it is well worth having for its winged stems and cheerful color. Another good easy broom is *G. dalmatica*. The leaves are spiny, but not ferocious, complicating weeding.

Gentiana acaulis: "Gorgeous deep blue trumpets in late spring. Creeping evergreen mats of rosette foliage." S. "Royal blue trumpet flowers in early spring." CA. Several subspecies of *G. acaulis* exist with different-sized leaves, usually from different locations in the Alps. Some people have had difficulty in finding the right place in the garden to produce the trumpets.

Gentiana scabra: "Usually producing procumbent stems with many large brilliant blue flowers in September and October. Wonderful draped over a rock." W. "An exquisite fall blooming gentian from Japan. Very late season, deep-blue flowers clustered at the stem tips making a striking scene set against fallen autumn leaves." S. "A fine October-blooming gentian with a somewhat candelabra-like pattern of growth. It should be allowed more than one season's growth to produce its lovely upturned flowers of blue." WR. All true, but in the Berkshires three factors must be reckoned with: leaves may cover the flowers; early frosts may damage them; deer are poised at the edge of the garden in search of *G. scabra*.

Gentiana septemfida: "Dark blue, late summer flowers in big clusters." S. "Narrow, bell-shaped, dark blue flowers form in terminal clusters." CA. There are gentians for all seasons, and this is about the best of the summer bloomers.

Geranium dalmaticum: "Mounds of shining green, aromatic leaves, tinted crimson in autumn, are smothered in clear-pink flowers in summer." S. " Plant this in a mostly sunny area with other mid-sized possessions." WR. There is also a white form. Give it plenty of space to make a carpet a yard across. Geraniums on the whole are overbearing in a rock garden, but this one is well behaved and lovely.

Geranium sanguineum is not to be let loose in a small garden, but there is a form 'Lancastriense' which is nearly allowable. "Pale pink flowers, 6" mat." C. "Light pink with darker veins." WR

Gypsophila cerastioides: "Low mounds of rounded velvety leaves. In summer large white cup-shaped flowers striped pink. Best in rich scree or trough." S.

Gypsophila repens: "Creeping Baby's breath has multitudes of quarter-inch flowers and blooms for weeks in late spring" R. "Dainty pink flowers." RK. Normally white, good forms are pink, but not often a very strong color. "Low haze of pink...effective in a cascading position." WR.

Helianthemum nummularium: "Delightful flowers display in sunny colors." S. Most of the species helianthemums are yellow. This species is very variable and scores of color forms are available. The leaves, too, can vary from green to grey. They also vary in hardiness, and you may want to take cuttings of the ones you are fond of. In any case a given plant is unlikely to last more than two seasons, but they are so colorful that it is worth trying to keep them. Allow at least one to two feet across for final size.

Hepatica: "Some of the most beautiful and earliest of spring flowering plants for rich leaf mold soil in the woodland garden. Good drainage is a must." S. " Very early in spring the blue or white blossoms emerge and open in the sun." R. There are two North American species *H. americana* ("Leaves with rounded lobes often mottled." W.) and *H. acutiloba* (" Evergreen leaves with three sharply pointed lobes." W.), which seem to differ only in leaf shape. There are many variations in form. *H. nobilis* is the European species; it has bigger flowers and more varieties. Rarer is *H. transylvanica* and its hybrid *H.* x *ballardii*. Any one of them could be tried in a shady rock garden, even though a woodland setting is more like home.

Heuchera hallii: "A petite alpine from Pikes Peak in Colorado. Slender stems of tiny white bells above little 1" leaves." S. The border coral bells look wrong in a rock garden, and the larger species are better at the edge of a woodland garden, but there are a few suitable alpine species. It doesn't mind sun.

Hippocrepis comosa: "Heads of yellow pea-like blooms are generously produced on a flat mat of green pinnate foliage." WR.

Houstonia caerulea: "Sun or part shade; good soil. Tiny tufts of evergreen leaves; solitary rather large pale to medium blue flowers on long stalks; blooms primarily in April or May, but at least in the South, sporadically all year." W. For us it grows wild in full sun, grass meadow, poor soil. Bluets, or Quaker Ladies, is delightful. If you move a good color form into the garden it fades away, seeming to prefer the crowded meadow.

Hylomecon japonicum: "Early spring yellow poppies. Elegant pinnate leaves. A beautiful herbaceous perennial native to Japanese woodlands." S. It resembles *Chelidonium majus*, the weedy celandine poppy, but is shorter, prettier, fewer flowers and not weedy.

Hymenoxys acaulis: "Rocky mountain native with dense tufts of silky, woolly leaves." CA. This lovely yellow composite is not always a "beginner's plant"—there are so many forms from high alpine to tubby Great Plains kinds. If it lives and blooms through its first summer, collect seed and sow it next winter.

Hypoxis hirsuta: "Yellow Star Grass. Sun or part shade; ordinary loam." W. An *Iris* relative like a small yellow *Sisyrinchium*.

Iberis saxatilis: "Dense mat 2-3" tall." CA. I like all the *Iberis* I have ever grown.

Iberis sempervirens: "Mounds of white in spring and deep green masses the rest of the year are indispensable in the rock garden." R. Candytuft white is bright and clean, making this a very useful foil for too busy or too drab color schemes.

Iris cristata: "A woodland dwarf from eastern America. Running habit in loose humusy soil. Deciduous." S. "Sky-blue flowers on 4" stems." R. "Give it a little sun and well drained soil." M. "Should form nice little drifts in a hurry." WR Usually blue. Many color forms have been selected including a vigorous white. It will tolerate a rock garden but wants to run around and prefers the edge of the woodland. If it has good roots, plant it with the rhizome top showing above ground. If the root system is weak, plant it slightly covered to keep it stable. The rhizome has to be horizontal.

Lavandula angustifolia: Lavenders are good shrub substitutes in a small rock garden, especially in their miniature forms. In time they grow too bulky, so keep them trimmed back and neat-looking during the spring clean-up.

Leontopodium alpinum: "Grey-green foliage covered with woolly hair bears thick, white woolly bracts on 10" stems. European classic." CA. Everybody has to grow edelweiss at least once to impress one's non-gardening friends. If you like it, go on to the more refined *L. nivale* and many other species.

Lewisia cotyledon: "Our glorious native is considered one of the best. Striking fleshy leaves often crinkled or notched. Numerous spring flowers in a rainbow of possible seedling colors (pink, white, orange, salmon) often candy-striped. Needs perfect drainage, grit around the crown. Afternoon shade of rocks." S. "Grow in humus and grit. Likes part shade and acid soil." R. "Likes well-drained soil or scree. Avoid winter wet." CA. You must try out many places in your garden if at first you are unsuccessful. When you find the right spot, expect an unimagined burst of pride and pleasure.

Lilium pumilum: "The coral lily is a delightful, small plant suitable for a rock garden. It blooms in late spring with small, scarlet Turk's cap flowers and does well in sun or part shade. One-and-a-half-feet tall." M. This is one of the few lilies that look well in a rock garden, but you have to remember that even a small lily is a large plant compared with the mats and buns that predominate. Place it with this in mind.

Linum capitatum: "A robust and free-flowering species from the mountains of Bulgaria. Dense heads of sizable rich yellow flowers." S.

Linum flavum: "Sunny yellow flowers and lush broad-leaved foliage make this a notable plant in late spring." R.

Lithodora oleifolia: "A splendid wanderer from the Pyrenees with tufts of hairy grey-green leaves spreading by underground stolons. Pink buds open to large opalescent blue flowers. Quite hardy in loose, rich, neutral to lime soil. Zone 5." S. When you first see *L. diffusa* 'Grace Ward' you will certainly want to grow it for its rich blue flowers. It is tender in my climate but occasionally worth a one-year stand. *L. oleifolia* is a more faithful companion.

Mentha requieni: "Purple, moss-like, aromatic. Moist soil or part-shade, half-hardy." NG. This is a tiny mint from Corsica with the most delicious smell when you crush the leaves or walk on it. It nearly always comes back each spring, even though not really hardy, either by self sowing or by stoloniferous roots which survive.

Mitchella repens: "This beautiful native plant is a wonderful ground cover in shaded rock gardens or woodland areas. It blooms in spring with pairs of small, white flowers followed by red berries. The dark green leaves are a delight throughout the year. Zones 3-8." M. "Small leather-like dark green leaves with a paler mid-vein; charming paired white flowers densely pubescent inside." W. "Partridge-berry is a wee creeper that slowly forms a flat-as-a-pancake patch in a woodsy, shady, slightly acid site." WR. Wild in our woods.

Orostachys iwarenge: "Bouquet of grey roses sitting flat on the ground." RK.

Orostachys aggregatum: "Succulent rosettes somewhere between pea and jade green." WR.

Orostachys furusei: "Spreading blue rosettes that send up smokestacks of dusty rose flowers in October. It doesn't look hardy but it is. From Japan." R. Ohwi (*Flora of Japan*) says these plants are different and should be called sedums. Perhaps they look more like sempervivums. They get a lot of attention in flower, though you could hardly call them flamboyant.

Orostachys spinosum: "Intricately scaled, heavily spined globes, up to 2" across" R. The spines are not very frightening and the flower stem is phallic. Unlike *O. furusei*, this doesn't spread by stolons. The rosette that flowers will die, but usually there are offsets that grow to make a larger plant next season.

Papaver miyabeanum: "Japanese. Related to the Iceland poppy but more heat tolerant. Grey-green basal leaves; beautiful delicate white flowers." W. "Lemon yellow flowers over interesting compact foliage." CA This poppy is in the *nudicaule* group, usually a low growing plant.

Penstemon davidsonii: "Creeping evergreen mats. Small round leaves. Lavender to purple from the California Sierras." S. The most permanent of the penstemons are the 'shrubby' group. The stems are woody and the leaves try to stay green all winter but often lose the battle to cold winds. Don't cut off the damaged stems until after flowering. The plants usually recover their good looks exactly at flowering time. A handkerchief of spun polyester spread over a plant and held down with stones helps with the winter-kill problem.

Penstemon fruticosus: "Miniature evergreen shrublet." R. "6-12" tall with blue to lavender flowers." CA. Another shrubby penstemon with many forms. Some of them can be bushes two feet across. On the whole easier than most members of this group.

Penstemon hirsutus 'Pygmaeus': "Rosettes of summer green and winter bronze foliage as well as violet flowers in spring." M. "A little guy with smokey-mauve blossoms on compact 5-6" stems." WR. This is one of the eastern penstemons (non-woody). Seedlings are likely to appear and may yield plants which look like the tall form of *P. hirsutus*.

Phlox amoena: "This native phlox produces vivid, deep pink flowers in mid-spring. The decumbent stems are lined with somewhat hairy, slender leaves which turn a lovely purple red in winter. Sun or part shade. 6"." M.

Phlox bifida: "Dainty, starry flowers of palest blue. Native Midwestern species is enchanting." R. "A dome covered in early summer by large lavender-blue flowers with deep-cut petals like perfect snowflakes. Zone 4." S. "8-10" mound of spiny foliage." CA. "A fantastic species." WR. This makes a mound or mat as big as *P. subulata* and can be treated in much the same way.

Phlox divaricata: "The eastern American woodland phlox. Branchlets spread and root to form colonies." S. " Woodland phlox makes running clumps of blue in streamside woods. Sweetly fragrant flowers in clusters for weeks in spring. Grow in rich soil in shade or sun." R. "Indispensable in the spring garden." M. You could have this in a rock garden but only for a short time. It needs the full run of a woodland to seed and spread. Many color forms, but the ordinary blue is probably the best.

Phlox stolonifera: "The creeping woodland phlox from the US east coast." S. "Abundant clusters of long-tubed blossoms adorning 6-8" stems." WR. Again best where it can spread in a woodland clearing. Choose one of the good color selections; the species has a duller color.

Phlox subulata: "Prostrate mats smothered in late April to May with showy flowers." RK. My favorite species amongst the "common" phloxes. Go to town selecting good colors and leaf forms. The word *subulata* means prickly (actually awl-shaped), but some of the forms and crosses have gentler foliage. Some people allow seedlings to flourish in the lawn and gain a convincing wild look to that stretch of garden; this stands a certain amount of mowing and foot traffic. If you have a very tidy mind you may not want the garden to spill over in this way. We have this phlox with thymes, too, much nicer than weedy grass, and by now beyond control. Several hybrids of unknown parentage, but probably including *P. subulata*, go under the name *P. douglasii*.

Potentilla verna 'Nana': "Sun; rockery. Tight buns of lustrous bright green evergreen foliage. Bright yellow flowers in early spring." W. (=*P. tabernaemontana*)

Primula acaulis: "Flowers borne singly on 3" stems keep succeeding one another for weeks." R. This is the primrose. Not as easy to keep as the showy polyanthas but much more elegant. Its correct name is now *Primula vulgaris*: "The English primrose. Pale yellow, fragrant, early." C.

Primula denticulata: "The drumstick primrose. The early appearance of flower buds means that occasionally the very first ones are caught by late frosts. Put it in a protected position in shade in either a very wet or average garden soil." M. "Spherical heads of crowded purple flowers on stout 12" stems." CA. There are some strong violet-reds and pale lilac-blues and a good white. The first buds nestle low down amongst the leaves and gradually grow to as much as a foot high as the flowers open.

Primula japonica: "This is a beautiful, late spring-flowering species which has flower stalks to two and a half feet. It requires considerable moisture to bloom well with 1-6 superimposed, many-flowered umbels." M. You can use it in the woodland, but it likes to be near water. It is the easiest of the candelabra primroses. If your plants self-sow, they will produce all colors from red-on-the-blue-side to white. If they don't, they are probably not happy enough to stay very long at all.

Primula x *pruhoniciana* (former name is x *Juliana*): The *Juliana* are hybrids of *P. juliae* and should display its stoloniferous habit. "Relatively small plants with dark green crinkly foliage and good sized flowers." CA. The crosses can be with *P. vulgaris*, in which case there would be only one flower on a stem, or with *P. elatior* or *P. veris* (or *P. polyantha*), in which case there would be multiple heads. Give them a shady place rather than the rough and tumble of a woodland to get them established. Later you can move chunks to the woods. In any case, division after two or three years is needed to keep plants flowering well. Primulas respond to fresh ground and feeding.

Ptilotrichum spinosum: "A shrubby *Alyssum* relative. Densely branched and spiny shrub covered in a haze of rosy flowers in early summer." S. "Shrubby domes of wiry silver stems, just two or three inches high. Rosy pink flowers in summer." R. The word shrub needn't scare you—this is just a low mound only a foot across. The color you get from seed is off-white, and it pays to get a 'Roseum' form if you want a brighter color.

Pulsatilla vulgaris: "Pasque flowers usher in spring. Their huge purple goblets are furry on the outside and close at night. On bright April days, before the leaves are on the trees, their blossoms will amaze you with their determined insistence that spring is here!" R. "These anemone relatives emerge in late winter as furry buds that open to big satiny goblets with golden stamens. Then the leaves unfold and the flowers become long-lasting fluffy seed heads which are quite showy." S. "Exquisite, chalice-shaped purple flowers. Decorative fluffy seed heads." W. All the rhapsodies about pulsatillas are warranted.

Sanguinaria canadensis: "Pure white single flowers in the spring. Woodland." C. "Ethereal 2-4" flowers, white with yellow centers; attractive broad-lobed leaves last all summer." W. "An early spring delight as the striking white blossoms appear on stems that are clasped in the unfurled leaf." WR. The lovely bloodroot only lasts a few days, but it is so exquisite that it should be in every garden. Besides, the leaves are elegant masterpieces.

Saponaria ocymoides: "Pink spreading flowers late May-June. Easy. Bright." RK. Good mat-forming and easy going.

Saponaria x *olivana*: "A crisp clump of bright green leaves, about 2-3" high, with showy bright pink flowers that lay out flat on the ground, tightly around the exterior of the plant." WR. Another reliable soapwort.

Saxifraga x *apiculata*: "Closely packed cushion made up of half-inch rosettes. Yellow clustered flowers on three-inch stems. The easiest Kabschia saxifrage to grow in the garden." R. "Crisp foliage and an inflorescence of primrose yellow flowers on compact 2" stems." WR. Most of the porophylla section of *Saxifraga* (kabschias) flower too early, grow too slowly, or display too much temperament to grow in the open garden. Give them container conditions with cold-frame protection. This one is reliable outside.

Saxifraga: Mossy section. These plants are common enough in England, but many gardeners in the Northeast find them troublesome. I feel they are worth trying, and if and when they produce the brown patches that disfigure the mats after blooming and after winter, you can root cuttings in a sandy mix quite easily. Some people step on them to get the stems in contact with the soil and claim they will root in place, but I have had no such experience. 'Peter Pan' is a good one: "Vivid crimson flowers in spring." S.

Saxifraga paniculata: The silver saxifrages are the easiest and most satisfying for permanence. This species covers many forms and subspecies. All are suitable for any rock garden but better if you can avoid full sun all day. "Clumping mounds of silvery green foliage with white to pale cream flowers." CA.

Sedum cauticola: "It has rounded succulent leaves, wants part shade, and produces rosy-pink flowers several weeks before those of its cousin, *S. sieboldii*." M. "Ascending stems with broad grey-green leaves; erect inflorescences of rose-purple flowers in early autumn." W. "Picturesque rock plants with deep greyish-blue leaves and near-ruby red flowers." WR.

Sedum kamschaticum: "Semi-evergreen mat-forming species from Northeast Asia; lax stems with rather thin, spatulate, bright green leaves; large, yellow flowers in mid-summer." W.

Sedum pluricaule: A well-behaved and handsome sedum.

Sedum spathulifolium: Some forms of this West Coast native are a bit tender for me, and they all get damaged by very cold, exposed conditions. It is probably OK in S. Connecticut though, and all forms are very beautiful.

Sempervivum arachnoideum: "Heavily webbed white in spring." RK. "Compact button-like rosettes with a white web. The more sun you give them the stronger the webbing will be." WR.

Silene schafta: "Long blooming from May to September." RK. This plant has the same "value" as *Saponaria ocymoides* and is a standard in everybody's garden. It may self-sow and need a little discipline.

Silene virginica: "Sun or light shade; good drainage. Spectacular plant; rosettes of evergreen leaves; branched stems bearing 1 1/2" to 2" flowers with brilliant scarlet, bi-lobed petals; blooms for long period in spring." W.

Thymus lanuginosus: Introduce thymes into your rock garden with great circumspection. This one is woolly and slower than most. If you love them, try to clear a sunny bank just for their benefit and find companion plants that can compete.

Tiarella wherryi: "Pink flowered foamflower that stays in a clump. Has more pointed, palmate leaves than *T. cordifolia*." R. Whether or not you lump these two species you may still want this form. Grow it in woodland or a very shady place.

Trillium grandiflorum: "Queen of the spring woodland all over the east. Large snowy flowers produced in abundance on a mature plant are breathtaking." R.

Veronica armena: "Small charming plant only 2" tall, with radiating stems. Produces small loose sprays of gentian-blue flowers in mid-summer." CA. "Deeply divided leaves and bright blue blooms." WR. Some veronicas are a bit weedy, but this is quite well-behaved

Veronica prostrata: "Makes a deep green carpet that bursts forth with cobalt blue flowers in early summer." S. "Beautiful patch of long lasting color in June." R. There are white, pink, and blue forms of this mat-forming plant.

Viola labradorica: "This native violet has beautiful dark purple leaves throughout most of the year and small violet flowers for much of the summer. It is compact and not invasive." M. It is difficult to recommend any easy violets, because they are all more or less invasive. This one produces such small plants that they are not too destructive, and you can pull them out if they are in the way. The only violets not to fear are the impossible-to-grow ones from the Rockies and the Alps.

Viola pedata. "About the showiest violet and one of the showiest wildflowers; flattish inch-wide (or larger) blue purple flowers; dissected leaves. " W. Some people find this spreads around. We have found it a good violet.

Vitaliana primuliflora (syn. *Douglasia vitaliana*): Lovely mat of hard silver-green foliage with yellow flowers just after the drabas have gone over. "Clear yellow flowers on a carpet of grey-green leaves." R.

The nurseries mentioned are not the only sources for these plants. I want to thank them for allowing me to quote from their catalogs. Here is a list of nurseries quoted, in operation in 1994:

Siskiyou Rare Plant Nursery, Dept 1, 2825 Cummings Rd, Medford, OR 97501
Rice Creek Nursery no longer sells mail-order
Montrose Nursery has closed
Cricklewood Nursery, 11907 Nevers Road, Snohomish, WA 98290
We-Du Nurseries, Rte.5, Box 724, Marion, NC 28752-9338
Rocknoll Nursery in operation under new management
Woodland Rockery, 6210 Klam Rd, Otter Lake, MI 48464
Colorado Alpines,Inc., P.O.Box 2708, Avon, CO 81620; no longer sells mail-order
Nature's Garden, 40611 HWY 226, Scio, Oregon 97374

Postscript: Aftercare
What do you do when the plants you have ordered by mail arrive? Here are a few suggestions. There are no fixed rules to follow because there are too many variables: the nursery of origin, the size of the plant, its state of health, and most of all your own facilities. However, you must assume that the plant that has traveled by air has all the potential ills that you might have on your first flight; it could be dehydrated, hungry, travel-sick, jet-lagged, and just plain tired. It also could be very young and possibly ill.

If you have nowhere to put it except in the garden then do something like the following. Bare root plants: for shrubs and trees half-fill a bucket with water, and set the roots in water for several hours. For a small plant use a vase or a cup. Put the container outside in a shady spot if the weather is warm; if it is really cold, try a porch or somewhere cool indoors. Plants must not freeze or boil or bake—common sense obviously—but you would be surprised how easy it is to forget that the sun moves, nights get cold, furnaces kick on, etc. Overnight is not too long for a shrub or a wilted plant to sit in water, and since UPS arrives in the afternoon, overnight is a good idea for most plants.

Treat alpines and small perennials as you would a transplant of your own seedlings. Have prepared a container of compost and several clean pots of different sizes. The compost should be a mix of "what works best for you": I would use fifty percent soilless peat-based compost and fifty percent coarse sand, with a good helping of slow release fertilizer. There would be nothing wrong with adding soil or leaf mold and varying the proportions. You must remember that the aim is to get the plant actively growing again, so the mix should be airy, moist but not soggy, and contain nutrients. Also, the plant will be planted out in the garden before long. This means the compost must be compatible with your soil. There is no point in coaxing a plant to start regrowth in a mixture heavily laced with perlite if you are then going to plant it out in a garden of heavy clay. Nor should you overdo the sand if the ultimate planting out place is a leafy woodland.

Plants already in compost: many plants arrive with something clinging to their roots which will be wrapped in foil, plastic, newspaper, or some other material that holds the whole together. You should shake off the loose material and find out whether the roots are actually growing in it, or whether the material is merely for protection. Protective material, usually peat, may hide the fact that the roots are folded over or bunched up in an unnatural way and need to be spread out before planting. Don't incorporate the dry peat with your own compost, as it may throw the texture out of balance and decrease wetability. If the roots are in fact growing in the medium, it is more than likely they were taken from a rootbound pot and are bunched up. Straighten out the root ends, trim off the broken pieces, use judgment about how much growing medium to retain, and plant on in an adequately large pot—one big enough to hold the roots comfortably spread out—but not so large that the plant "drowns" in soil. "Almost pot-bound" is about right. You may have to trim off an unusually long root, but this requires great discretion and even greater courage.

If the plant is still in its container: you could knock it out and discard loose compost from the rootball and replant it in a slightly larger pot if needed. If the plant looks perfectly happy (I mean not hopelessly pot-bound or loosely planted) in its pot, leave it there.

When the plants have been repotted, stand them in an inch of water and leave them overnight. Next day, take them outside into a shady place and leave them there for a week or so before you plant them in the garden. Even if you have to delay planting out they should be fine for weeks, but they may need more sun and water. I think it is a waste of time to plant out real invalids or plants that are too small, so find a protected home for these orphans. What is "big enough" and "healthy enough" to plant out is a matter of judgment accumulated over years of failures and successes. Don't expect a hundred percent success rate with any shipment.

If you have nowhere to put plants except in the garden (you may not have a holding place or even a work place; or the roots of a bare-root plant may be larger than you can accommodate in any of your store of used pots), it is imperative to cover them with an upturned pot or bucket to protect them from sun and harsh weather. Since these will be left in place until the plant shows signs of new life or dies, the pots will need a stone to hold them in place. By the end of the shipping season you will be thoroughly tired of looking at a garden full of upturned plant pots.

In general, discard as much imported soil or compost as is compatible with the health of the plant. It will be a different compost from the one you use and may carry pests, slug eggs, diseases (not likely but it has happened), and weed seeds, moss, liverwort, or other weeds (this very often happens). This advice is even more important if you are going to keep the plant in an alpine house, as the whole house could become infected. Be ruthless in destroying liverwort. Many gardens have been disfigured by this pest being inadvertently or carelessly introduced from a nursery. Remember that during their busiest season a nursery may not be able to weed every plant before shipping, so you have to be prepared for Good and Evil to arrive together by UPS and take necessary precautions.

Starting a Nursery

If you are thinking of going into the nursery business and have a strong interest in growing rock garden plants to sell, there are a few points to bear in mind. This is not a list of "basic plants" in the sense that every rock gardener should grow them. It is a selection of plants available through mail-order catalogs in 1994. Some of these plants will always be favorites, but most of them are available for only two or three years and then side-lined for a few years before being revived at a later date. A good list should have a strong element of change in order to keep customers happy. Gardeners want novelty, which sometimes implies rarity, and a list with unique offerings is very attractive.

The other danger in having a list that is too static is that gardeners, being generous people, share their plants with others, so a plant that is easy to propagate for you is going to saturate the market at a great rate. This happened with plants like *Anemonella* 'Shoaf's Double' and will probably happen with *Corydalis flexuosa* 'Blue Panda.' But the plants that "everybody seems to have" will be lost by the majority of gardeners, who are normal, busy, careless unprofessionals, and the plants will eventually become collector's items again in the future. Now the *Anemonella* has become a rarity again. Difficult but growable plants like *Porophyllum* saxifrages or Asiatic gentians will always be in demand. Especially popular are good clones or special forms, and rock gardeners are as susceptible to names like 'Beauty of Denver' or 'Panayoti's Pleasure' as any other gardener.

Modified with permission from *A Gardener Obsessed*, David R. Godine: Boston. 1994.

Geoffrey Charlesworth, author of The Opinionated Gardener *and* A Gardener Obsessed, *is one of the most articulate writers and experienced growers in the Society. He gardens in Sandisfield, Massachusetts.*

Resources

by Jack Ferreri

CORE BOOKS

Rock Gardening in America: A Guide to Growing Alpines and Other Wildflowers in the American Garden by H. Lincoln Foster (1968, reprinted several times)
Written some thirty years ago by America's foremost rock gardener, this volume wears its age exceedingly well. The finest explanation of the fundamentals of rock gardening technique, as well as a full, entertaining list of plants to grow. The best first book for newcomers.

Cuttings from a Rock Garden by H. Lincoln Foster (1990)
A splendid collection of "Linc's" writings for the Society's Bulletin and other publications. Especially strong on Eastern woodlanders, but filled with wonderful general gardening reflections, as well.. The volume includes photos of his legendary Millstream Garden and features the world-class illustrations done by Linc's wife Laura Louise Foster ("Timmy").

The Opinionated Gardener (1988) and *A Gardener Obsessed* (1994)
by Geoffrey Charlesworth
The author brings together vast growing experience, a whimsical sense of humor, and entertaining writing to elevate the rock gardening essay to new heights. His fluency as a writer makes you forget just how skilled a grower he is. Both books are delightful collections of informative, inspiring, and enjoyable essays.

Bernard E. Harkness Seedlist Handbook, 2rd Edition (1993)
The first place to look for the basic information on a plant … height, blossom color, origin, and where to find a photo. Compiled dutifully from the Seed Exchange listings of the major rock gardening societies since the early seventies. Updated in 1993 by Mabel Harkness. Also on-line.

Rock Gardens (1997)
Part of the New York Botanical Gardens' "The Serious Gardener" Series. A sumptuously-illustrated guide to growing alpines, focusing on the NYBG's T.H. Everett Rock Garden. Features excellent information on a wide range of cultural topics (sand beds, stone selection, gardening in different parts of the country, etc.).

The AGS Encyclopedia by Alpine Garden Society. (1994)
Mammoth two-volume illustrated compendium of alpine and rock garden plants. Very expensive to own, but a joy to leaf through. Perhaps the most informative single listing of alpine plants.

A SELECTION OF BOOKS ON SPECIFIC TOPICS

Any large general – purpose bookstore will carry many books of interest to rock gardeners. What follows is a very selected and necessarily very personal compilation of books which a developing rock gardener will find good use for.

A Manual of Alpine and Rock Garden Plants by Christopher Grey-Wilson

Alpines by Will Ingwersen

Alpines in the Open Garden by Jack Elliott

Alpines: The Illustrated Dictionary by Clives Jones

Bulbs for the Rock Garden by Jack Elliott

Campanulas and Bellflowers in Cultivation by Clifford Crook

Campanulas by Peter Lewis & Margaret Lynch

Daphne by C.D. Brickell and Brian Mathew

The English Rock Garden by Reginald Farrer

The Genus Androsace by George Smith and Duncan Lowe

The Genus Gentiana by Josef Halda

A Guide to Rock Gardening by Richard Bird

Jewels of the Plains by Claude Barr

Manual of Alpine Plants by Will Ingwersen

Primula by John Richards

The Rock Garden and its Plants by Graham Stuart Thomas

Rock Garden Plants of North America by NARGS

Rock Garden Plants: a Color Encyclopedia by B. Mineo

Rock Gardens by Wilhelm Schacht

Rock Gardens Through the Year by Karl Foerster

Rocky Mountain Alpines by NARGS

The Smaller Bulbs by Brian Mathew

The Smaller Rhododendrons by Peter Cox

Handbook on Troughs by NARGS

ADDITIONAL RESOURCES: WEBSITES

There are hundreds of websites of interest, created and maintained by botanical gardens, horticultural institutions, nurseries or expert plantsmen. Many sites offer excellent color pictures. There you may learn about thousands of plants, and sometimes where to buy them or get seeds.

NARGS maintains its own website which offers a storehouse of information on our organization, other societies and rock gardening in general. It has an extensive list of useful links. Do visit it at : www.nargs.org